The BEST Thing About 'Jelly Rolls'... They are Sugar–Free

12 Great Quilts with 'Jelly Rolls' or 2¹/₂" Strips

Heritage Bouquet

pieced Janice Irick
quilted by Julie Lawson

Gorgeous flowers in sumptuous colors enliven your décor and present a wonderful opportunity to showcase all your needle skills. This prize-worthy design offers a creative collection of sampler blocks surrounding a beautiful appliqué center which is then framed by strip rows and multiple borders.

This fabulous quilt is surprisingly simple to assemble and is destined to be a treasured part of your family heritage.

FABRIC USED: "Heritage, Cause for the Cure" by Howard Marcus

instructions on pages 21 - 27

Redbirds

pieced Janice Irick
quilted by Susan Corbett

Cardinal song wafts on gentle breezes, through the open windows of your summer cottage and into your heart. Make a quilt that celebrates the joys our feathered friends bring to our lives, homes and neighborhoods.

This charming sampler is packed with simple techniques and easy piecing that will please both beginners and experienced quilters.

FABRIC: "Redbirds in the Bowers" by Debbie Schmitz

instructions on pages 28 - 34

Time in the Garden

pieced by Kayleen Allen
appliqued by Janice Irick
quilted by Julie Lawson

Soothing soft tones give this quilt an inviting, comfortable feel. The block border is wonderfully simple to piece and the applique shapes are fun to do.

These muted shades complement any decor so this quilt will be a lovely gift for anyone on your list.

FABRIC USED: "Portobello Market" by 3 Sisters

instructions on pages 34 - 39

Our Town

pieced by Donna Arends Hansen
quilted by Sue Needle

Home Sweet Home! Perfect for teaching a Block of the Month class for beginner quilters, this fun sampler offers four different house blocks, five pieced traditional blocks and an easy applique.

The fabric collection gives this project a wonderful Americana feel that complements every decor.

FABRIC USED: "American Primer"
by Minick & Simpson

instructions on pages 40 - 45

Strip-Samplers

Hometown Houses

pieced by Donna Perrotta
quilted by Julie Lawson

From New York to Los Angeles, Chicago to Houston, big cities beckon to millions of adventurous Americans with promise of a life that throbs to a faster beat. As any inhabitant of Manhattan or New Orleans will proudly proclaim, their hometown is the best place in the world. Capture the excitement with a fabulous cityscape quilt of your own.

FABRIC USED: "Wildflower Serenade" by Kansas Troubles

instructions on pages 46 - 49

Favorite Things

pieced by Donna Hansen
quilted by Julie Lawson

Raindrops on roses and whiskers on kittens..
this delightful sampler offers all your favorite
things for the heart and home as well as subjects
from your garden.

Our scotty dog won't bite and this quilt will
keep you so warm, you won't need mittens.

FABRIC USED: "Recess" by American Jane

instructions on pages 50 - 57

Home Garden

pieced by Betty Nowlin

quilted by Julie Lawson

When the sunlight grows warm and the frosts disappear, you know it's time to plant your favorite flowers.

Grow a garden of springtime cheer in your sewing room this winter and you'll be ready to welcome the first zephyrs of the season.

FABRIC USED:
"Butterfly Fling"
by Me & My Sister

instructions
on pages 58 - 59

Butterfly Blocks

pieced by Kayleen Allen
quilted by Julie Lawson

Give your traditional Courthouse Steps a kick!
Gorgeous colors frame fussy-cut butterfly blocks
in a tilted setting that is so simple to sew!
Create a fresh look with this great technique.

FABRIC: "Butterfly Fling" by Me & My Sister

instructions on pages 60 - 61

Fruit Salad

pieced by Donna Perrotta
quilted by Julie Lawson

Luscious fruits combine in a cool summer treat. Fruit Salad is a favorite summer snack and this little quilt is great for that special picnic in the park, at the beach, or in the backyard.

Since you will likely find the kids 'borrowing' this quilt from the front porch swing, you might want to make two.

FABRIC USED: "Recipe for Friendship" by Mary Engelbreit

instructions on pages 62 - 67

Pie, Oh My!

pieced by Kayleen Allen
appliqued by Edna Summers
quilted by Julie Lawson

What's your favorite pie? Whether it's apple, cherry, or strawberry, you'll enjoy the delicious delights of a calorie-free quilting experience.

Basic block construction and fabulous fabrics make this quilt a tempting treat for everyone who loves something sweet at bedtime.

FABRIC USED: "Recipe for Friendship" by Mary Engelbreit

instructions on pages 68 - 71

Table Runner

pieced by Donna Arends Hansen
quilted by Sue Needle

Invite your family and guests to your table or buffet sideboard with a lovely runner. Cozy houses meet the market square on a wonderful small project.

This simple design is easily adapted in any color palette and is perfect for showing off your seasonal prints.

Table runners make welcome gifts and add that designer touch that softens a room.

FABRIC USED:
"Portobello Market" by 3 Sisters

instructions on pages 19 - 20

SIZE: 22" x 62"

YARDAGE:
Yardage is given for using either fabric yardage
    or 'Jelly Roll' strips.
We used a *Moda* "Portobello Market" by 3 Sisters
    'Jelly Roll' collection of 2½" fabric strips
    - we purchased 1 'Jelly Roll'

4 strips	OR	⅓ yard Ivory
2 strips	OR	⅙ yard Brown
2 strips	OR	⅙ yard Light Blue
2 strips	OR	⅙ yard Red
2 strips	OR	⅙ yard Green
1 strip	OR	⅛ yard Tan

Center Square & Roofs   Purchase ⅙ yard Red print
Sashing, Border, Binding   Purchase 1 yard Steel Blue
Backing   Purchase 1½ yards
Batting   Purchase 30" x 70"
Sewing machine, needle, thread

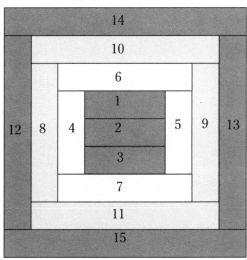

Block B - Center Square

BLOCK B:
CUTTING CHART

Quantity	Length		Position
Tan	2	10½"	#6, 7
	2	6½"	#4, 5
Light Blue	2	14½"	#10, 11
	2	10½"	#8, 9
Red	2	18½"	#14, 15
	2	14½"	#12, 13
	3	6½"	#1, 2, 3

BLOCK B: CENTER SQUARE
Refer to the Block Assembly Diagram.
    Sew 1-2-3. Press.
    Sew 4 and 5 to the left and right sides of the piece. Press.
    Sew 6 and 7 to the top and bottom of the piece. Press.
    Sew 8 and 9 to the left and right sides of the piece. Press.
    Sew 10 and 11 to the top and bottom of the piece. Press.
    Sew 12 and 13 to the left and right sides of the piece.
        Press.
    Sew 14 and 15 to the top and bottom of the piece. Press.

SASHING STRIPS:
    Cut 4 strips 2½" x 18½".
    Sew a strip to the top and bottom of center block B. Press.

Table Runner

photo is on page 18

PREPARATION FOR STRIPS:
    Cut all strips 2½" by the width of fabric (usually 42" - 44").
    Label the stacks or pieces as you cut.

SORTING: Sort 2½" strips into stacks:

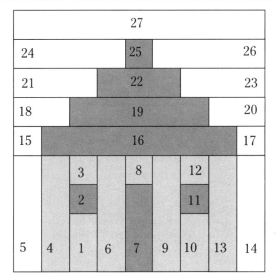

Block A - House with Red Door

BLOCK A:
CUTTING CHART

Quantity		Length	Position
Green	4	8½"	#4, 6, 9, 13
	2	4½"	#1, 10
	3	2½"	#3, 8, 12
Red	1	14½"	#16
	1	10½"	#19
	2	6½"	#7, 22
	3	2½"	#2, 11, 25
Ivory	1	18½"	#27
	4	8½"	#5, 14, 24, 26
	2	6½"	#21, 23
	2	4½"	#18, 20
	2	2½"	#15, 17

BLOCK A: HOUSE WITH RED DOOR
Refer to the Block Assembly Diagram.
House Unit: Sew 1-2-3. Press.
    Sew 4 and 5 to the left side of the piece. Press.
    Sew 6 to the right side of the piece. Press.
    Sew 7-8 together. Press.
    Sew 7-8 to the right side of the piece. Press.
    Sew 9 to the right side of the piece. Press.
    Sew 10-11-12. Press.
    Sew to the right side of the piece. Press.
    Sew 13 and 14 to the right side of piece. Press.
Roof Unit: Sew 15-16-17. Press.
    Sew 18-19-20. Press.
    Sew 21-22-23. Press.
    Sew 24-25-26. Press.
    Sew the roof rows together.
    Sew #27 to the top of the roof. Press.
    Sew roof section to the top of house unit. Press.
Sashing: Sew a 2½" x 18½" strip to bottom of house
    block A. Press.

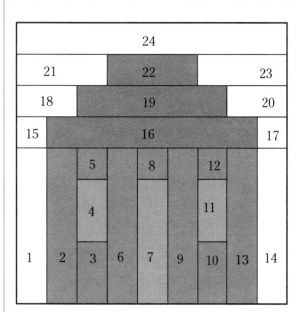

Block C
House with Blue Door

BLOCK C:
CUTTING CHART

Quantity		Length	Position
Ivory	1	18½"	#24
	2	10½"	#1, 14
	2	6½"	#21, 23
	2	4½"	#18, 20
	2	2½"	#15, 17
Brown	4	10½"	#2, 6, 9, 13
	2	4½"	#3, 10
	3	2½"	#5, 8, 12
Red	1	14½"	#16
	1	10½"	#19
	1	6½"	#22
Med Blue	1	8½"	#7
	2	4½"	#4, 11

BLOCK C:

HOUSE WITH BLUE DOOR
Refer to the Block Assembly Diagram.
House section: Sew 1-2. Press.
   Sew 3-4-5. Press.
   Sew 1-2 to 3-4-5. Press.
   Sew 6 to the right side of the piece. Press.
   Sew 7-8. Press.
   Sew 7-8 and 9 to the right side of the piece. Press.
   Sew 10-11-12. Press.
   Sew 10-11-12 to the right side of the piece. Press.
   Sew 13 and 14 to the right side of the piece. Press.
Roof section: Sew 15-16-17. Press.
   Sew 18-19-20. Press.
   Sew 21-22-23. Press.
   Sew the roof rows together. Press.
   Sew the roof section to the top of the house.
      Press.
Sashing: Sew a 2½" x 18½" strip to bottom of house
   block C. Press.

Town Square Table Runner
Assembly Diagram

ASSEMBLY:
   Referring to assembly diagram, sew blocks
      together. Press.
Border:
   Cut 2 strips 2½" x 62½" for sides.
   Sew side borders to the quilt. Press.

FINISHING:
Quilting: See Basic Instructions.
Binding: Cut strips 2½" wide.
      Sew together end to end to equal 180".
      See Binding Instructions.

The Mitered Border instructions are for the "Our Town" quilt pictured on pages 10 -11.

Mitered Border

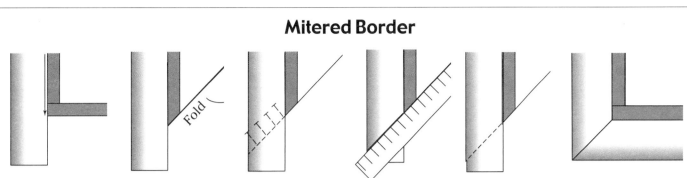

| Center, pin and sew borders to the sides of the quilt. Stop the seam at the corner. | Fold the quilt at a diagonal so the miter will extend from the corner outward. | Pin or baste miter seam, carefully line up the pattern. | Use a ruler to draw a line from the corner out to the edge of the border. Sew a seam. TIP: I use a long stitch in case I need to rip it out and redo it. | Check the miter seam to be sure it lines up correctly and lays down flat, resew it with a normal stitch. | Trim off excess fabric underneath the corners. Repeat on all 4 corners. |

Heritage Bouquet

photo on pages 4 - 5

SIZE: 56" x 74"
TIP: Add more borders to make a larger quilt.

YARDAGE:
Yardage is given for using either fabric yardage
    or 'Jelly Roll' strips.
We used a *Moda* "Heritage" by Howard Marcus
    'Jelly Roll' collection of $2\frac{1}{2}$" fabric strips
    - we purchased 1 'Jelly Roll'

7 strips	OR	$\frac{1}{2}$ yard Dark Brown
6 strips	OR	$\frac{1}{2}$ yard Medium Brown
6 strips	OR	$\frac{1}{2}$ yard Tan
4 strips	OR	$\frac{1}{3}$ yard Dark Blue Gray
3 strips	OR	$\frac{1}{4}$ yard Light Blue Gray
1 strip	OR	$\frac{1}{8}$ yard Paisley or print
2 strips	OR	$\frac{1}{6}$ yard Rose
2 strips	OR	$\frac{1}{6}$ yard Ivory

Ivory Center Block	Purchase $\frac{5}{8}$ yard
Brown print Border #4	Purchase $\frac{3}{8}$ yard
Border #5 & Binding	Purchase $1\frac{7}{8}$ yards
Backing	Purchase $3\frac{5}{8}$ yards
Batting	Purchase 64" x 82"

Sewing machine, needle, thread
DMC Brown pearl cotton or 6-ply floss for stems
#22 or #24 chenille needle

PREPARATION FOR STRIPS:
    Cut all strips $2\frac{1}{2}$" by the width of fabric
        (usually 42" - 44").
    Label the stacks or pieces as you cut.

SORTING:
    Sort the following $2\frac{1}{2}$" strips into stacks:

POSITION	QUANTITY & COLOR
Blocks A & D	3 Light Blue Gray
Blocks A, B, E, F, J, L, P, S	6 Medium Brown
Blocks A, B, F, H, I, J, L, P, R	6 Tan
Applique, Blocks B, G, I, K, M, R	4 Dark Blue Gray
Applique, Blocks C, H, O, Q, T	2 Rose
Blocks D, H, K, M, N, Q, S, & Border #3	7 Dark Brown
Applique, Blocks E, N	1 Paisley
Blocks C, E, G, O, Q, T	2 Ivory

CENTER: Cut 1 Ivory $18\frac{1}{2}$" x $24\frac{1}{2}$".
APPLIQUE:
    Refer to the Applique instructions.
    Cut out applique pieces from patterns.
    Applique as desired.
    Embroider stems with along and short Running stitch.

SAMPLER BLOCK ASSEMBLY:
Refer to Chart and instructions for each block.
Label each piece as you cut.
Each finished block measures 6½" x 6½".

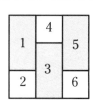

BLOCK C:
CUTTING CHART

Color	Quantity	Length	Position
Rose	3	4½"	#1, 3, 5
Ivory	3	2½"	#2, 4, 6

BLOCK C ASSEMBLY:
Column 1: Sew #1-2. Press.
Column 2: Sew #3-4. Press.
Column 3: Sew #5-6. Press.
    Sew the columns together. Press.

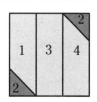

BLOCK D:
CUTTING CHART

Color	Quantity	Length	Position
Light Blue Gray	3	6½"	#1, 3, 4
Dark Brown	2	2½	#2

BLOCK D ASSEMBLY:
Refer to the Snowball Corners diagram.
Columns 1 & 3: Align a Dark Brown square with one end of #1 & #4.
Sew on the diagonal and fold back the flap as shown. Press.
Refer to the Block D diagram.
Sew the columns together. Press.

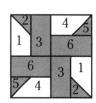

BLOCK E:
CUTTING CHART

Color	Quantity	Length	Position
Paisley or print	2	2" x 3½"	#3
	2	2" x 2"	#2
Ivory	4	2" x 3½"	#1, 4
Medium Brown	2	2" x 3½"	#6
	2	2" x 2"	#5

BLOCK E ASSEMBLY:
Refer to the Snowball Corners diagram.
Align a Paisley square #2 on the end of Ivory #1.
Sew the diagonal and fold back the flap. Press. Make 2.
Repeat for the remaining Ivory strips using Brown squares. Press.
Sew #1-2 to #3. Press. Make 2.
Sew #4-5 to #6. Press. Make 2.
Arrange the squares following the Block E diagram.
Sew the squares together in 2 rows, 2 squares per row. Press.
Sew the rows together. Press.

Snowball Corners Diagram

BLOCK F:
CUTTING CHART

Color	Quantity	Length	Position
Tan	2	4½"	#1, 5
	1	2½"	#4
Medium Brown	1	4½"	#3
	2	2½"	#2, 6

BLOCK F ASSEMBLY:
Row 1: Sew #1-2. Press.
Row 2: Sew #3-4. Press.
Row 3: Sew #5-6. Press.
    Sew the rows together. Press.

BLOCK G:
CUTTING CHART

Color	Quantity	Length	Position
Ivory	3	6½"	#1, 3, 4
Dark Blue Gray	4	2½"	#2

BLOCK G ASSEMBLY:
Refer to the Snowball Corners diagram.
Align a square with each end of #1 and #4.
Sew on the diagonal and fold back the flap as shown. Press.
Refer to the Block G diagram.
Sew the columns together. Press.

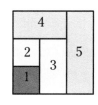

BLOCK H:
CUTTING CHART

Color	Quantity	Length	Position
Dark Brown	1	2½"	#1
Tan	1	2½"	#2
	1	4½"	#3
Rose	1	4½"	#4
	1	6½"	#5

BLOCK H ASSEMBLY:
Sew #1-2. Press.
Sew #3 to the right side of the piece. Press.
Sew #4 to the top of the piece. Press.
Sew #5 to the right side of the piece. Press.

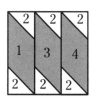

BLOCK I:
CUTTING CHART

Color	Quantity	Length	Position
Tan	2	6½"	#4, 5
	1	2½"	#2
Dark Blue Gray	2	2½"	#1, 3

BLOCK I ASSEMBLY:
Sew #1-2-3. Press.
Sew #4 & #5 to the top and bottom of the piece. Press.

BLOCK J:
CUTTING CHART

Color	Quantity	Length	Position
Medium Brown	3	6½"	#1, 3, 4
Tan	6	2½"	#2

BLOCK J ASSEMBLY:
Refer to the Snowball Corners diagram.
Align a square on each end of #1, #3 and #4.
Note the direction of the diagonal and sew on the
    diagonal line. Fold back the flap. Press.
Sew the columns together. Press.

BLOCK K:
CUTTING CHART

Color	Quantity	Length	Position
Dark Blue Gray	3	6½"	#1, 3, 4
Dark Brown	4	2½	#2

BLOCK K ASSEMBLY:
Refer to the Snowball Corners diagram on page 2.
Align a square with each end of #1 and #4.
Sew on the diagonal and fold back the flap as shown. Press.
Refer to the Block K diagram.
Sew the columns together. Press.

BLOCK L:
CUTTING CHART

Color	Quantity	Length	Position
Tan	1	6½"	#2
	1	5"	Unit 1, 3
Medium Brown	2	5"	Unit 1, 3

BLOCK L ASSEMBLY:
Refer to the Units diagram.
Sew 5" strips Brown-Tan-Brown to make a piece 5" x 6½". Press.
Cut the piece into 2 strips 2½" x 6½".
Sew the columns together. Press.

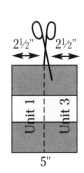

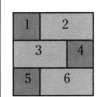

BLOCK M:
CUTTING CHART

Color	Quantity	Length	Position
Dark Blue Gray	3	4½"	#2, 3, 6
Dark Brown	3	2½"	#1, 4, 5

BLOCK M ASSEMBLY:
Row 1: Sew #1-2. Press.
Row 2: Sew #3-4. Press.
Row 3: Sew #5-6. Press.
    Sew the rows together. Press.

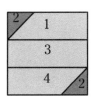

BLOCK N:
CUTTING CHART

Color	Quantity	Length	Position
Paisley or print	3	6½"	#1, 3, 4
Dark Brown	2	2½"	#2

BLOCK N ASSEMBLY:
Refer to the Snowball Corners diagram.
Rows 1 & 3: Align a Dark Brown square with one end
    of #1 & #4.
Sew on the diagonal and fold back the flap as shown.
    Press.
Refer to the Block N diagram.
Sew the rows together. Press.

BLOCK O:
CUTTING CHART

Color	Quantity	Length	Position
Rose	2	6½"	#1, 3
Ivory	1	6½"	#2

BLOCK O ASSEMBLY:
Sew the rows together. Press.

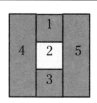

BLOCK P:
CUTTING CHART

Color	Quantity	Length	Position
Medium Brown	2	6½"	#4, 5
	2	2½"	#1, 3
Tan	1	2½"	#2

BLOCK P ASSEMBLY:
Sew #1-2-3 together. Press.
Sew the columns. Press.

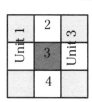

BLOCK Q:
CUTTING CHART

Color	Quantity	Length	Position
Rose	2	5"	Unit 1, 3
Dark Brown	1	2½"	#3
Ivory	1	5"	Unit 1, 3
	2	2½"	#2, 4

BLOCK Q ASSEMBLY:
Refer to the Units diagram.
Sew 5" strips
    Rose-Ivory-Rose to make a piece
    5" x 6½". Press.
Cut the piece into 2 strips
    2½" x 6½".
Row 2: Sew squares #2-3-4 together.
    Press.
Sew the columns together. Press.

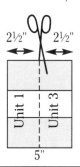

BLOCK R:
CUTTING CHART

Color	Quantity	Length	Position
Tan	2	6½"	#1, 3
Dark Blue Gray	1	6½"	#2

BLOCK R ASSEMBLY:
Sew #1-2-3. Press.

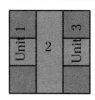

BLOCK S:
CUTTING CHART

Color	Quantity	Length	Position
Dark Brown	2	5"	Unit 1, 3
Medium Brown	1	6½"	#2
	1	5"	Unit 1, 3

BLOCK S ASSEMBLY:
Refer to the Units diagram.
Sew 5" strips
    Dark Brown-Medium Brown-Dark
    Brown to make a piece 5" x 6½".
    Press.
Cut the piece into 2 strips 2½" x 6½".
Sew the columns. Press.

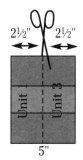

BLOCK T:
CUTTING CHART

Color	Quantity	Length	Position
Rose	3	6½"	#1, 3, 4
Ivory	6	2½"	#2

BLOCK T ASSEMBLY:
Refer to the Snowball Corners diagram.
Align a square on each end of #1, #3 and #4.
Note the direction of the diagonal and sew on the
    diagonal line. Fold back the flap. Press.
Sew the rows together. Press.

You will love these blocks. They are all done with a really quick-piecing method. The center took some time but now you will be able to work quickly to complete the quilt top.

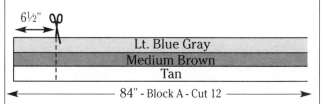

BLOCK A:
Use 2 strips each of Light Blue Gray, Medium Brown, Tan.
Sew 2 strips (per color) end to end to make a strip
    about 84" long of each color.
Refer to the Block A diagram.
Sew the strips together side by side:
    Light Blue Gray - Brown - Tan
    to make a piece 6½" x 84". Press.
Cut the piece into 12 sections, each 6½" x 6½".
Label these Block A.

BLOCK B:
Repeat instructions for Block A using
    2 strips each of Dark Blue Gray, Medium Brown
    and Tan.
Sew 2 strips (per color) end to end to make a strip 84"
    long of each color.
Refer to the Block A diagram.
Sew the strips together side by side: Dark Blue Gray-
    Brown - Tan to make a piece 6½" x 84". Press.
Cut the piece into 12 sections, each 6½" x 6½".
Label these Block B.

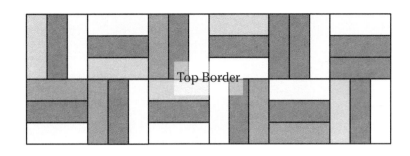

Top Border

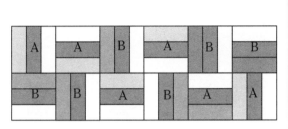

A-B Blocks - Top Border

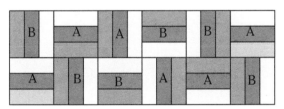

A-B Blocks - Bottom Border

A-B BORDER ASSEMBLY:
Refer to the A-B Block Border diagrams for direction and placement.

Top Row 1: Sew A-A-B-A-B-B. Press.
Top Row 2: Sew B-B-A-B-A-A. Press.

Sew the rows together. Press.
Label as Top Border. Set aside.

Bottom Row 1: Sew B-A-A-B-B-A. Press.
Bottom Row 2: Sew A-B-B-A-A-B. Press.

Sew the rows together. Press.
Label as Bottom Border. Set aside.

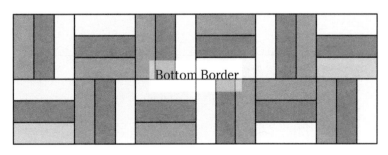

Bottom Border

Sampler Block Border #1:
Left side: Sew Blocks I-J-K. Press.
Right side: Sew Blocks L-M-N. Press.
Sew the sides to the center piece. Press.
Top: Sew Blocks C-D-E-F-G-H. Press.
Bottom: Sew Blocks O-P-Q-R-S-T. Press.
Sew the top and bottom to the center piece. Press.

A-B Border #2:
Sew the top and bottom A-B borders to the quilt. Press.

Heritage Bouquet - Quilt Assembly Diagram

BORDERS:

Dark Brown Pieced Border #3:
Sew strips together end to end. Press.
    Cut 2 strips 2½" x 54½" for sides.
    Cut 2 strips 2½" x 40½" for top and bottom.
    Sew side borders to the quilt. Press.
    Sew top and bottom borders to the quilt. Press.

Border #4:
Cut strips 2½" by the width of fabric.
Sew strips together end to end.
    Cut 2 strips 2½" x 58½" for sides.
    Cut 2 strips 2½" x 44½" for top and bottom.
    Sew side borders to the quilt. Press.
    Sew top and bottom borders to the quilt. Press.

Border #5:
Cut strips 6½" wide parallel to the selvage to eliminate piecing.
    Cut 2 strips 6½" x 62½" for sides.
    Cut 2 strips 6½" x 56½" for top and bottom.
    Sew side borders to the quilt. Press.
    Sew top and bottom borders to the quilt. Press.

FINISHING:
Quilting:
    See Basic Instructions.
Binding:
    Cut strips 2½" wide.
    Sew together end to end to equal 270".
    See Binding Instructions.

Note: This quilt is also available as a pattern pack
    #0950 "Heritage Bouquet" by Design Originals.

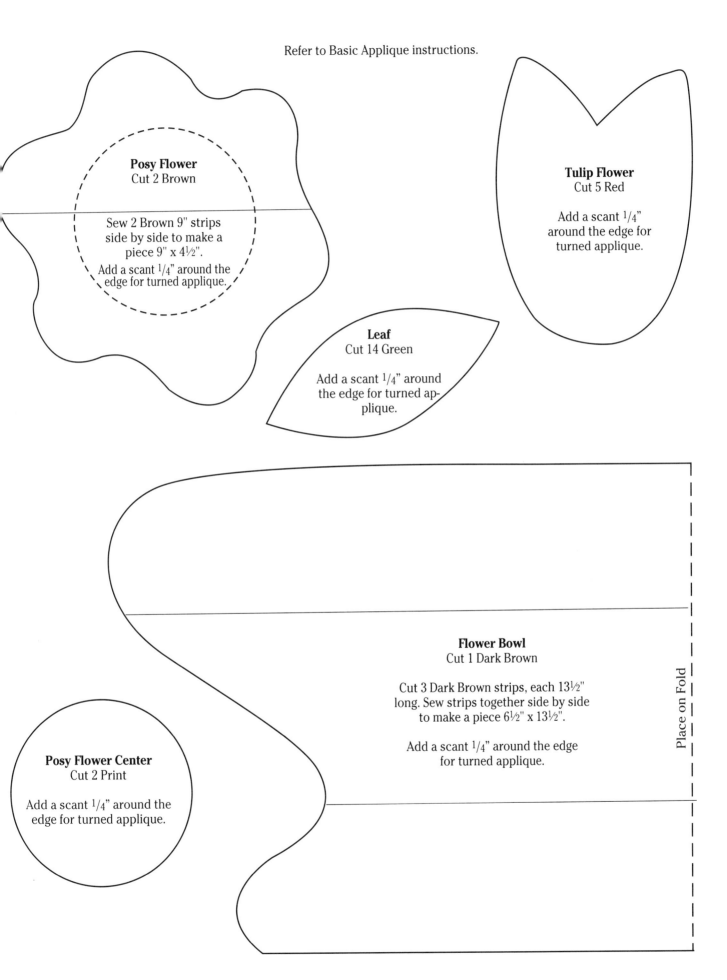

Refer to Basic Applique instructions.

Posy Flower
Cut 2 Brown

Sew 2 Brown 9" strips side by side to make a piece 9" x 4½".

Add a scant ¼" around the edge for turned applique.

Tulip Flower
Cut 5 Red

Add a scant ¼" around the edge for turned applique.

Leaf
Cut 14 Green

Add a scant ¼" around the edge for turned applique.

Flower Bowl
Cut 1 Dark Brown

Cut 3 Dark Brown strips, each 13½" long. Sew strips together side by side to make a piece 6½" x 13½".

Add a scant ¼" around the edge for turned applique.

Place on Fold

Posy Flower Center
Cut 2 Print

Add a scant ¼" around the edge for turned applique.

Redbirds

photo is on pages 6-7

SIZE: 58" x 80"
TIP: Add more borders to make a larger quilt.

YARDAGE:
Yardage is given for using either fabric yardage
　　or 'Jelly Roll' strips.
We used a *Moda* "Redbird in the Bowers" by Kathy Schmitz
　　'Jelly Roll' collection of 2½" fabric strips
　　- we purchased 1 'Jelly Roll'

5 strips	OR	⅜ yard Cream
3 strips	OR	¼ yard Gold
7 strips	OR	½ yard Red
8 strips	OR	⅝ yard Blue
4 strips	OR	⅓ yard Dk. Green
7 strips	OR	½ yard Brown

Background	Purchase 1 yard Cream
Border #1	Purchase ½ yard Brown Print
Border #2 & Binding	Purchase 2 yards Red Print
Backing	Purchase 5 yards
Batting	Purchase 67" x 89"

Sewing machine, needle, thread
Optional: 10 size ⅜" black buttons for bird eyes

PREPARATION FOR STRIPS:
　　Cut all strips 2½" by the width of fabric
　　　　(usually 42" - 44").
　　Label the stacks or pieces as you cut.

SORTING:
　　Sort the following 2½" strips into stacks:

Background Cream Fabric
CUTTING CHART

Quantity	Length	Position
1	8½" x 26½"	Section 5 background
2	4½" x 16½"	Section 7 - #10, 13
3	26½"	Sashing: 2 of E, 1 of K
3	16½"	Sashing: T, Section 7 - #1, 4,
1	14½"	Section 7 - #2
1	12½"	Section 7 - #11
2	10½"	Sashing P
1	8½"	Sashing R
12	6½"	Sashing: 4 of A, 4 of G, 2 of M, Section 7 - #5, 9
4	4½"	Sashing: 2 of L, Section 7 – #6, 8
41	2½"	28 Cornerstones for Section 2 #c
		12 Cornerstones for Section 3 #c
		1 Cornerstone for Section 7 - #7

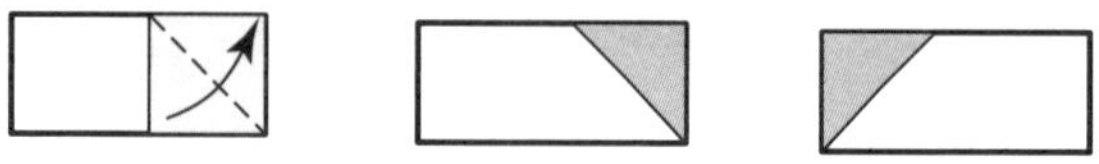

"Snowball" Corner Diagram

SNOWBALL CORNERS:
　　Some strips in the blocks use the "Snowball"
Corner technique. The direction of the diagonal for
each strip in the block varies, so you must carefully
note the diagonal on the block assembly diagram.
Some strips have a corner on only one end. The
squares used as "Snowball" Corners are labelled with
a "c" in the cutting list.
　　Tip: Fold back the triangle and check its position
before you sew.
　　Align a square with the appropriate end of the
strip and sew on the diagonal line. Fold the triangle
back and press before attaching it to any other strips.

Make 3

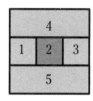

Block A - Make 3

Section 1 - Block A:
Make 3

CUTTING CHART

	Quantity	Length	Position
Red	3	2½"	#2
Gold	6	2½"	#1, 3
	6	6½"	#4, 5

ASSEMBLY - Make 1
　　Sew 1-2-3. Press.
　　Sew 4 to top of 1-2-3. Press.
　　Sew 5 to bottom of 1-2-3. Press.

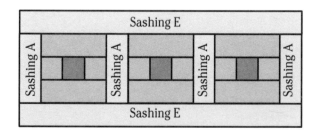

Section 1 - Assembly:
　　Sew a Sashing A – Block A - Sashing A – Block A –
　　　　Sashing A – Block A – Sashing A. Press
Top & Bottom Sashing:
　　Sew Sashing E to the top. Press
　　Sew another Sashing E to the bottom. Press

At this point, Section 1 should measure 10½" x 26½".

Section 2 – 'Flying Geese' Triangles:

CUTTING CHART

	Quantity	Length	Position
Red	14	4½"	B

You will need 28 of the 2½" Cream Corners - "c".

Section 2 - Flying Geese Assembly:
Make 14:
Position one Corner on one end of B.
Refer to "Snowball" Corner instructions to make a diagonal.
Position the second "c" Corner on the opposite end of B.
Refer to Snowball instructions to make the second diagonal.

Section 2 - Assembly:
Complete Section 2 by sewing a row of 13 of unit B together. Press.
(The one remaining Triangle unit will be used in Section 10.)

At this point, Section 2 should measure 4½" x 26½".

Make 3 of each   Block B - Make 3

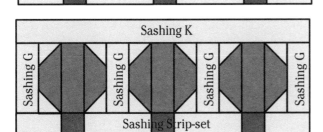

Sashing K

Sashing Strip-set

Section 3 – Tree Blocks:

CUTTING CHART

	Quantity	Length	Position
Dk. Green	9	6½"	N, O
Brown	3	2½"	D

Section 3 - Tree Blocks Assembly:
Make 3
Position a "c" Corner on each end of 6 N strips.
Refer to the Snowball Corner instructions to make a diagonal.
    Carefully note the direction of each diagonal to
    make 3 left and 3 right.
Sew N-O-N together side by side. Press.
    Carefully note the direction of each diagonal again.

Section 3 - Assembly:
Sew   Sashing G – Block B - Sashing G – Block B –
        Sashing G – Block B – Sashing G. Press
Sew   Sashing K to the top of Section 3. Press
Sew   Sashing L - D – Sashing M - D –
        Sashing M - D - Sashing L. Press
Sew this Sashing unit to bottom of Section 3. Press.

At this point, Section 3 should measure 10½" x 26½".

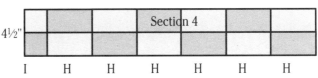

Make "Piano Keys" by cutting a
pair of strips into lengths.

4½"   cut 6 for H   2½"   cut 1 for I

Section 4

I   H   H   H   H   H   H

Section 4

CUTTING CHART

	Quantity	Length	Position
Gold	1	32"	strip for H
Cream	1	32"	strip for H

Sew a Cream Strip and a Gold Strip together side by
    side (Piano Keys) to make a Cream/Gold strip
    4½" x 32". Press
Cut across the 32" Cream/Gold strip to make
    6 strips of H, each 4½" long
    2 strips of I, each 2½" long
Sew I-H-H-H-H-H-H together alternating the
    colors in a checkerboard pattern. Press.
(The one remaining I unit will be used in Section 10.)
At this point, Section 4 should measure 4½" x 26½".

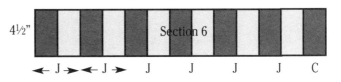

Section 6

← J → ← J →   J   J   J   J   C

Section 6 – Piano Keys:

CUTTING CHART

	Quantity	Length	Position
Brown	1	4½"	strip for C
	1	27"	strip for J
Cream	1	27"	strip for J

Sew a Cream Strip to a Brown Strip to make a
    Cream/Brown strip 4½" x 27". Press
Cut across the 27" length from Cream/Brown strips
    to make 6 strips of J, each 4½" long.
Sew J-J-J-J-J-C together alternating the colors.
    Start with Brown and end with Brown. Press.

At this point, Section 6 should measure 4½" x 26½".

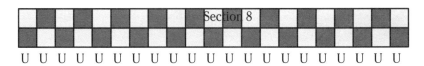

U U U U U U U U U U U U U U U U U U U U U

Section 8:
CUTTING CHART

	Quantity	Length		Quantity	Length
Brown	1	42½" strip	and	1	10" strip
Cream	1	42½" strip	and	1	10" strip

Sew a Cream Strip and a Brown Strip together side by side (Piano Keys) to make Cream/Brown strips 4½" x 42½" and 4½" x 10". Press.

Cut across the 42½" Cream/Brown strip to make. 21 strips of U, each 2½" x 4½" long.

Sew 21 of unit U together alternating the colors in a checkerboard pattern. Press.

At this point Section 8 should measure 4½" x 42½".

Section 7 – House Block:
CUTTING CHART

	Quantity	Length	Position
Brown	1	10½"	#16
	2	6½"	#15, 19
	1	4½"	#12
	3	2½"	#3, 14, 21
Red	1	10½"	#17
	3	6½"	#18, 20, 23
	1	4½"	#22
Dk. Green	2	9"	Small Tree appliqué
	3	10½"	Large Tree appliqué

You will also need Background Cream pieces for Section 7: #1, 2, 4, 5, 6, 7, 8, 9, 10, 11, 13

House: Sew 21 - 22. Press.
Sew 18 - 19 - 20 - 21/22 - 23. Press.
Sew 17 and 16 to the top. Press.

Roof: Sew 7 - 14. Press.
Sew 6 to the left and 8 to the right. Press.
Sew 15 to the bottom. Press.
Sew 5 to the left and 9 to the right. Press.'
Sew the roof to the house. Press.

Background: Sew 2 - 3. Press.
Sew 1 - 2/3 - 4. Press.
Sew this unit to the left of house. Press.
Sew 11 - 12. Press.
Sew 10 - 11/12 - 13. Press.
Sew this unit to the right of house. Press.

At this point Section 7 should measure 16½" x 26½".

Tree: Sew 2 Dark. Green 9" strips together side by side for the Small Tree appliqué. Press.
Sew 3 Dark Green 10½" strips together side by side for the Large Tree appliqué. Press.

Applique: Refer to the Applique instructions.

Section 9

W W W W W W W

Section 9
CUTTING CHART

	Quantity	Length	Position
Dk. Green	1	39"	strip for W
	1	6½"	
Cream	1	39"	strip for W
	1	6½"	

Sew a 6½" Dark Green and a 6½" Cream together side by side (Piano Keys) to make a Dark Green/Cream strip 4½" x 6½". Press.

Sew a 39" Dark Green and a 39" Cream together side by side to make a Dark Green/Cream strip 4½" x 39". Press.

Cut across the 39" Dark Green/Cream strip to make 6 strips of W, each 4½" x 6½" long.

Sew 7 units together alternating the colors in a checkerboard pattern. Press.

At this point Section 9 should measure 4½" x 42½".

Section 5

Section 5
CUTTING CHART

	Quantity	Length	Position
Red	2	4½"	Heart appliqué
	6	8½"	Large Redbird appliqué
Brown	2	4"	Large Redbird Wing appliqué
	2	2"	Large Redbird Head appliqué

You will also need 1 Background Cream 8½" x 26½".

Sew 2 Red 4½" strips together for Heart appliqué. Press.
Sew 3 Red 8½" strips together for Large Redbird. Make 2. Press.
Applique: Refer to the Applique instructions.

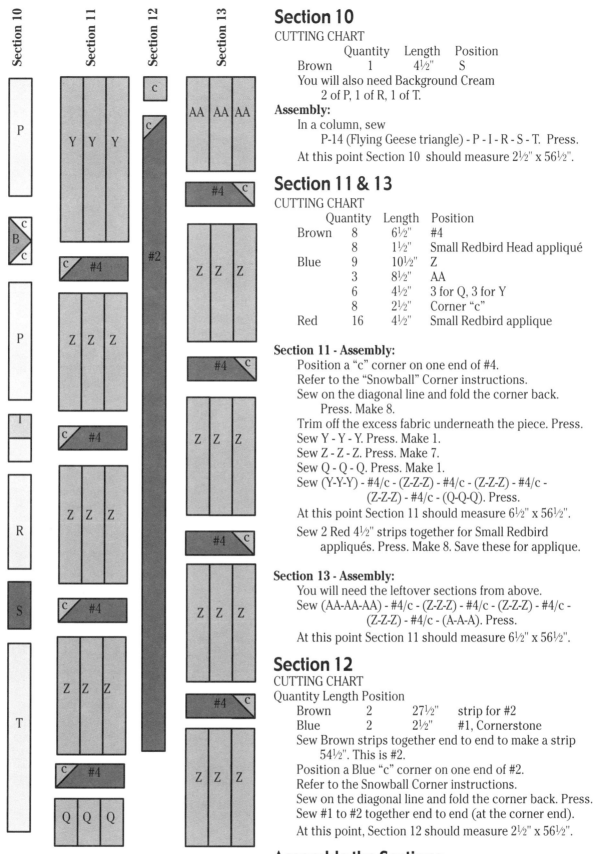

Section 10

CUTTING CHART

	Quantity	Length	Position
Brown	1	4½"	S

You will also need Background Cream
2 of P, 1 of R, 1 of T.

Assembly:
In a column, sew
P-14 (Flying Geese triangle) - P - I - R - S - T. Press.
At this point Section 10 should measure 2½" x 56½".

Section 11 & 13

CUTTING CHART

	Quantity	Length	Position
Brown	8	6½"	#4
	8	1½"	Small Redbird Head appliqué
Blue	9	10½"	Z
	3	8½"	AA
	6	4½"	3 for Q, 3 for Y
	8	2½"	Corner "c"
Red	16	4½"	Small Redbird applique

Section 11 - Assembly:
Position a "c" corner on one end of #4.
Refer to the "Snowball" Corner instructions.
Sew on the diagonal line and fold the corner back.
Press. Make 8.
Trim off the excess fabric underneath the piece. Press.
Sew Y - Y - Y. Press. Make 1.
Sew Z - Z - Z. Press. Make 7.
Sew Q - Q - Q. Press. Make 1.
Sew (Y-Y-Y) - #4/c - (Z-Z-Z) - #4/c - (Z-Z-Z) - #4/c -
(Z-Z-Z) - #4/c - (Q-Q-Q). Press.
At this point Section 11 should measure 6½" x 56½".

Sew 2 Red 4½" strips together for Small Redbird
appliqués. Press. Make 8. Save these for applique.

Section 13 - Assembly:
You will need the leftover sections from above.
Sew (AA-AA-AA) - #4/c - (Z-Z-Z) - #4/c - (Z-Z-Z) - #4/c -
(Z-Z-Z) - #4/c - (A-A-A). Press.
At this point Section 11 should measure 6½" x 56½".

Section 12

CUTTING CHART

Quantity	Length	Position
Brown	2	27½"	strip for #2
Blue	2	2½"	#1, Cornerstone

Sew Brown strips together end to end to make a strip
54½". This is #2.
Position a Blue "c" corner on one end of #2.
Refer to the Snowball Corner instructions.
Sew on the diagonal line and fold the corner back. Press.
Sew #1 to #2 together end to end (at the corner end).
At this point, Section 12 should measure 2½" x 56½".

Assemble the Sections

Sections 10 - 11 - 12 - 13
Assembly:
Sew Sections 10 - 11 - 12 - 13 together side by side. Press.

Applique: Refer to the Applique instructions.
At this point, the Section should measure 16½" x 56½".

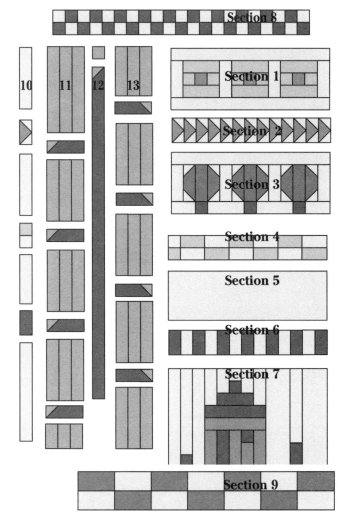

FINISHING THE QUILT TOP

Arrange all sections on a work surface or table.
Refer to diagram for section placement.

Sew Sections 1 - 2 - 3 - 4 - 5 - 6 - 7 together.
Press.

Sew the left Section to the right Section.
Press.

Sew Section 8 checkerboard to the top.
Press.

Sew Section 9 to the bottom.
Press.

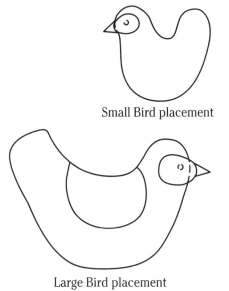

Small Bird placement

Large Bird placement

BORDERS:

Border #1:

Cut strips $2\frac{1}{2}$" by the width of fabric.
Sew strips together end to end. Press.
Cut 2 strips $2\frac{1}{2}$" x $64\frac{1}{2}$" for sides.
Cut 2 strips $2\frac{1}{2}$" x $46\frac{1}{2}$" for top and bottom.
Sew side borders to the quilt. Press
Sew top and bottom borders to the quilt. Press.

Border #2:

Cut strips $6\frac{1}{2}$" wide parallel to the selvage to
eliminate piecing.
Cut 2 strips $6\frac{1}{2}$" x $68\frac{1}{2}$" for sides.
Cut 2 strips $6\frac{1}{2}$" x $58\frac{1}{2}$" for top and bottom.
Sew side borders to the quilt. Press
Sew top and bottom borders to the quilt. Press.

APPLIQUE:

See Basic Appliqué instructions.
Cut out pieces from patterns.
Appliqué as desired.

FINISHING:

Quilting: See Basic Instructions.
Binding: Cut strips $2\frac{1}{2}$" wide.
Sew together end to end to equal 286".
See Binding Instructions.

Sew $\frac{3}{8}$" Black buttons for bird eyes.

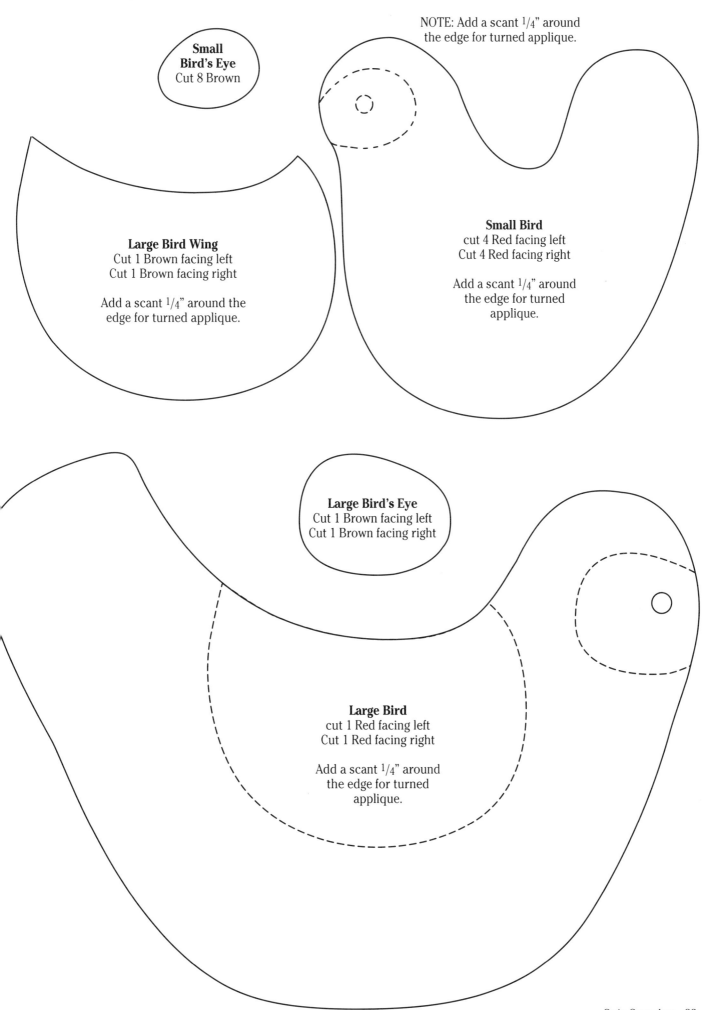

Small Bird's Eye
Cut 8 Brown

NOTE: Add a scant 1/4" around
the edge for turned applique.

Large Bird Wing
Cut 1 Brown facing left
Cut 1 Brown facing right

Add a scant 1/4" around the
edge for turned applique.

Small Bird
cut 4 Red facing left
Cut 4 Red facing right

Add a scant 1/4" around
the edge for turned
applique.

Large Bird's Eye
Cut 1 Brown facing left
Cut 1 Brown facing right

Large Bird
cut 1 Red facing left
Cut 1 Red facing right

Add a scant 1/4" around
the edge for turned
applique.

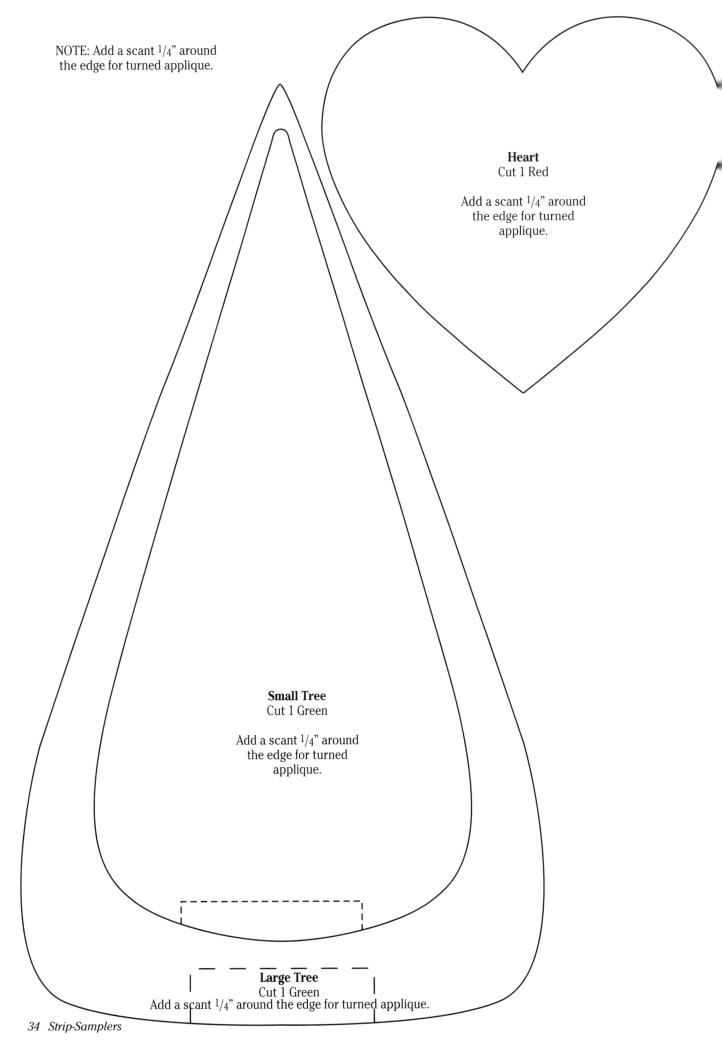

NOTE: Add a scant ¹/₄" around the edge for turned applique.

Heart
Cut 1 Red

Add a scant ¹/₄" around the edge for turned applique.

Small Tree
Cut 1 Green

Add a scant ¹/₄" around the edge for turned applique.

Large Tree
Cut 1 Green
Add a scant ¹/₄" around the edge for turned applique.

Time in the Garden

photo is on pages 8 - 9

SIZE: 58" x 66"
TIP: Add more borders to make a larger quilt.

YARDAGE:
Yardage is given for using either fabric yardage
or 'Jelly Roll' strips.
We used a *Moda* "Portobello Market" by 3 Sisters
'Jelly Roll' collection of 2½" fabric strips
- we purchased 1 'Jelly Roll'

7 strips	OR	½ yard Tan
6 strips	OR	½ yard Brown
6 strips	OR	½ yard Ivory
6 strips	OR	½ yard Red
5 strips	OR	⅜ yard Dark Blue
4 strips	OR	⅓ yard Light Blue
3 strips	OR	¼ yard Green

Quilt Center	Purchase 1 yard Ivory
Border #3 & Binding	Purchase ¾ yard Red
Border #4	Purchase 1⅔ yards Ivory print
Backing	Purchase 3½ yards
Batting	Purchase 66" x 74"

APPLIQUE FABRICS:
Bird beaks Purchase ⅛ yard Yellow or 1½" x 4½" scrap

Sewing machine, needle, thread
DMC pearl cotton or 6-ply floss
#22 or #24 chenille needle

PREPARATION FOR STRIPS:
Cut all strips 2½" by the width of fabric
(usually 42" - 44").
Label the stacks or pieces as you cut.

SORTING:
Sort the following 2½" strips into stacks:

POSITION	QUANTITY & COLOR
Block centers	4 Tan, 4 Ivory
Blocks A	4 Brown
Blocks B	4 Red
Blocks C	3 Dark Blue
Blocks D	3 Light Blue
Blocks E	2 Green
Appliques	2 Brown for rabbit
	1 Green for leaves
	2 Red for flowers & berries
	1 Light Blue & 2 Dark Blue for birds

CENTER:
Cut an Ivory rectangle 24½" x 32½".

APPLIQUE:
See Basic Applique instructions.
Cut out shapes using patterns.
Applique as desired.
Embroider stems with a long and short
Running Stitch.

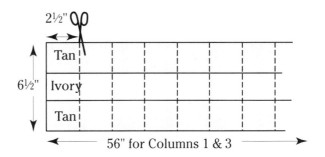

CHECKERBOARD CONSTRUCTION:
Columns 1 & 3:
Refer to the checkerboard assembly diagrams.
Sew 4 Tan strips together end to end.
Sew 4 Ivory strips together end to end.
Cut 1 Ivory and 2 Tan strips 2½" x 56".
Sew the strips together side by side Tan-Ivory-Tan
to make a piece 6½" x 56". Press.
Cut the piece into 22 strips 2½" x 6½".
Label 18 strips Column 1.
Label 4 strips Column 3.

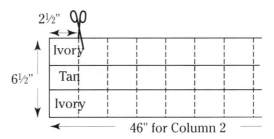

Column 2:
Cut 1 Tan and 2 Ivory strips 2½" x 46".
Sew the strips together side by side Ivory-Tan-Ivory
to make a piece 6½" x 46". Press.
Cut the piece into 18 strips 2½" x 6½".
Label them Column 2.

Column 1	Column 2	Column 3
T	I	T
I	T	I
T	I	T

Checkerboard Assembly
for Block A
Make 4

CHECKERBOARDS
FOR BLOCK A:

Checkerboards:
Refer to the Checkerboard
Block A diagram.
Arrange the pieces
in 3 columns each.
Sew the columns together.
Press.

Column 1	Column 2
T	I
I	T
T	I

Checkerboard Assembly
for Blocks B, C, D, E
Make 14

CHECKERBOARDS
FOR BLOCKS B, C, D, E:

Checkerboards:
Refer to the Checkerboard
Block B diagram.
Arrange the pieces
in 2 columns.
Sew the columns together.
Press.

BLOCK ASSEMBLY:
Block A:
For 4 Block A's, cut the
following Brown strips:
    eight 2½" x 10½",
    eight 2½" x 6½".
Sew a 6½" strip to the right and
    left sides of the center.
    Press.
Sew a 10½" strip to the top and
bottom of the center.
    Press. Make 4.

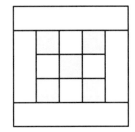

Block A - Make 4

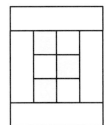

Block B - Make 5

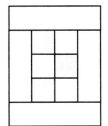

Block C - Make 3

Block B:
For 5 Block B's, cut the following Red strips:
    ten 2½" x 8½", ten 2½" x 6½".
Sew a 6½" strip to the right and left sides of the center.
    Press.
Sew an 8½" strip to the top and bottom of the center.
    Press. Make 5.

Block C:
For 3 Block C's, cut the following Dark Blue
    strips: six 2½" x 8½", six 2½" x 6½".
Sew a 6½" strip to the right and left sides of the center.
    Press.
Sew an 8½" strip to the top and bottom of the center.
    Press. Make 3.

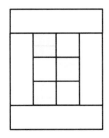

Block D
Make 4

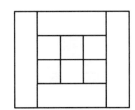

Block E
Make 2

Block D:
For 4 Block D's, cut the following Light Blue strips:
    eight 2½" x 8½", eight 2½" x 6½".
Sew a 6½" strip to the right and left sides of the center.
    Press.
Sew an 8½" strip to the top and bottom of the center.
    Press. Make 4.

Block E:
For 2 Block E's, cut the following Green strips:
    four 2½" x 8½", four 2½" x 6½".
Sew a 6½" strip to the right and left sides of the center.
    Press.
Sew an 8½" strip to the top and bottom of the center.
    Press. Make 2.

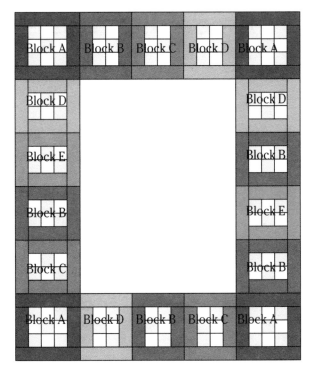

BLOCK BORDER ASSEMBLY:
    Arrange all blocks on a work surface or table.
    Refer to diagram for block placement and direction.
Left Side: Sew D-E-B-C. Press.
          Sew to the left side of quilt. Press.
Right Side: Sew D-B-E-B. Press.
          Sew to right side of quilt. Press.
Top: Sew A-B-C-D-A. Press.
          Sew to the top of the quilt. Press.
Bottom: Sew A-D-B-C-A. Press.
          Sew to the bottom of quilt. Press.

BORDERS:
Pieced Border #2:

Sides:
Cut 4 Tan and 4 Ivory strips 2½" x 13½".
    For the left side, sew Tan-Ivory-Tan-Ivory. Press.
    For the right side, sew Ivory-Tan-Ivory-Tan. Press.
    Refer to Assembly diagram for placement.
    Sew side borders to the quilt. Press.

Top:
Cut the following strips and sew them end to end in order:
    Tan 2½" x 17½"
    Ivory 2½" x 10½"
    Tan 2½" x 13½"
    Ivory 2½" x 8½"
    Sew to the top of the quilt. Press.

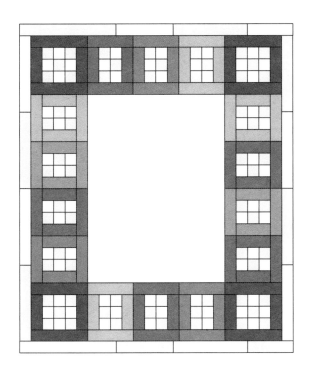

Time in the Garden - Quilt Assembly Diagram

Bottom:
Cut the following strips and sew them end to end in order:
- Ivory 2½" x 17½"
- Tan 2½" x 10½"
- Ivory 2½" x 13½"
- Tan 2½" x 8½"

Sew to the bottom of the quilt. Press.

Border #3:
Cut strips 1½" by the width of fabric.
Sew strips together end to end.
Cut 2 strips 1½" x 56½" for sides.
Cut 2 strips 1½" x 50½" for top and bottom.
Sew side borders to the quilt. Press.
Sew top and bottom borders to the quilt. Press.

Outer Border #4:
Cut strips 4½" wide parallel to the selvage to eliminate piecing.
Cut 2 strips 4½" x 58½" for sides.
Cut 2 strips 4½" x 58½" for top and bottom.
Sew side borders to the quilt. Press.
Sew top and bottom borders to the quilt. Press.

FINISHING:
Quilting: See Basic Instructions.
Binding: Cut strips 2½" wide.
Sew together end to end to equal 258".
See Binding Instructions.

Note: This quilt is also available as a pattern pack
#0952 "Time in the Garden" by Design Originals.

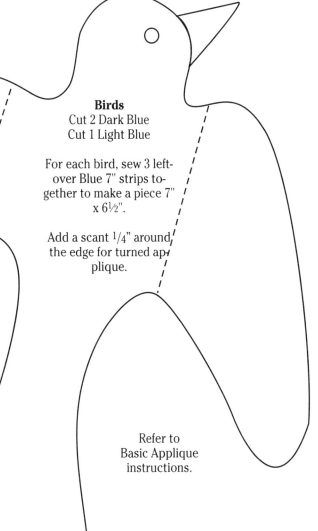

Birds
Cut 2 Dark Blue
Cut 1 Light Blue

For each bird, sew 3 left-over Blue 7" strips to-gether to make a piece 7" x 6½".

Add a scant ¼" around the edge for turned ap-plique.

Refer to
Basic Applique
instructions.

Join to tail section here

Refer to
Basic Applique
instructions.

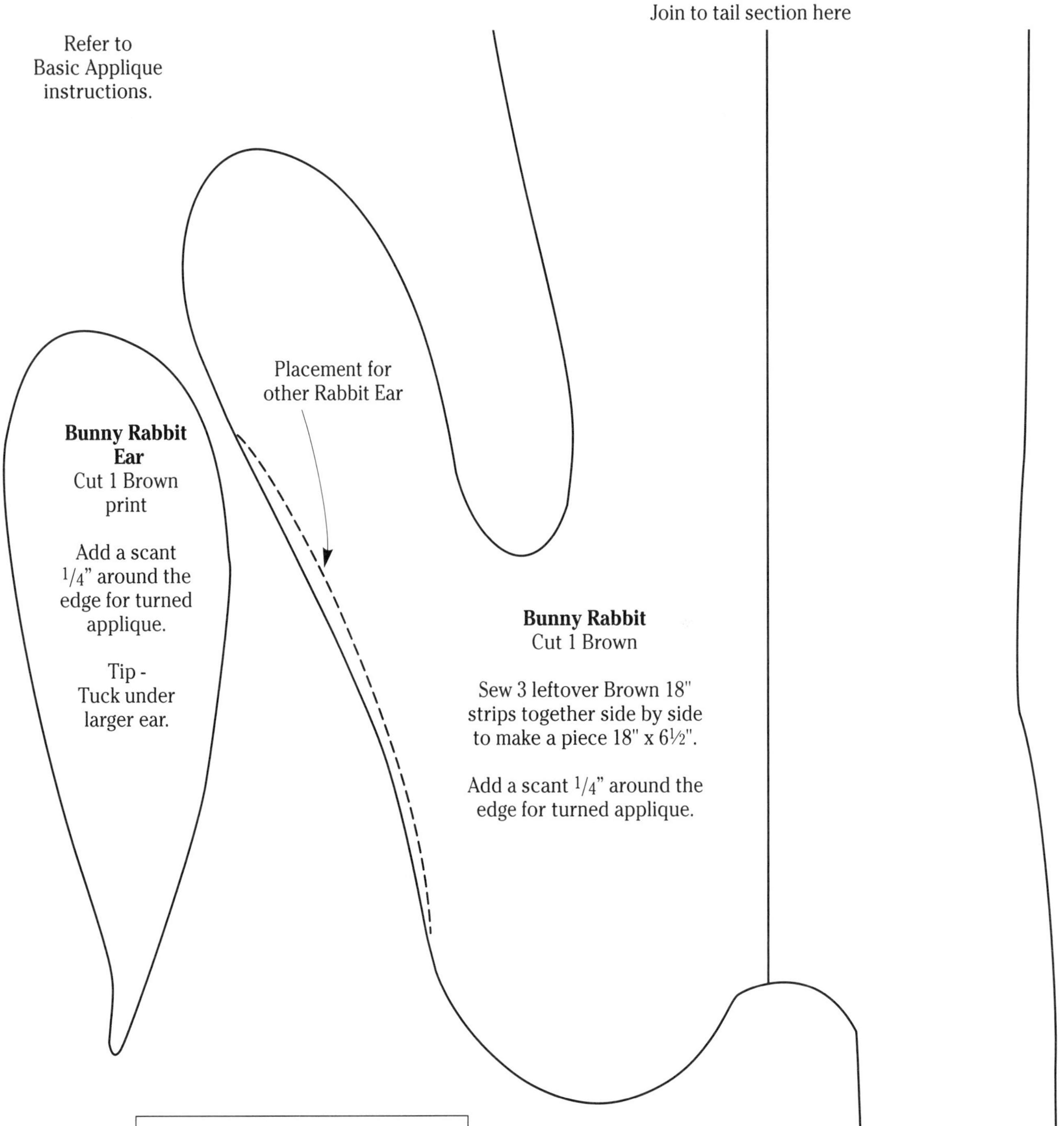

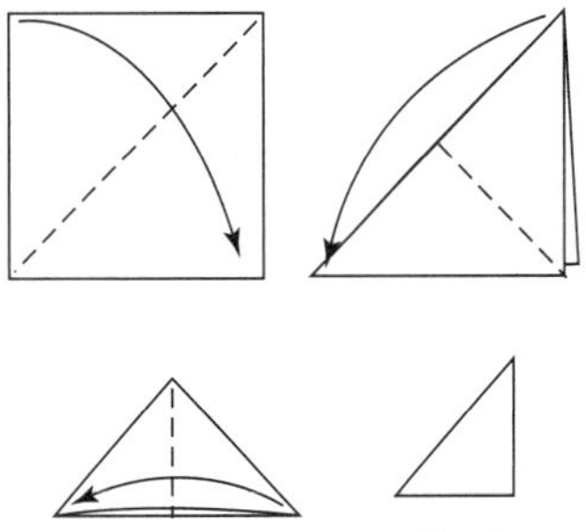

Placement for
other Rabbit Ear

**Bunny Rabbit
Ear**
Cut 1 Brown
print

Add a scant
1/4" around the
edge for turned
applique.

Tip -
Tuck under
larger ear.

Bunny Rabbit
Cut 1 Brown

Sew 3 leftover Brown 18"
strips together side by side
to make a piece 18" x 6½".

Add a scant 1/4" around the
edge for turned applique.

Beak

BIRD BEAK:
    For each beak, cut a Yellow
1½" square and fold it 3 or 4 times
into the desired beak shape.
    Position under the bird and ap-
plique in place.

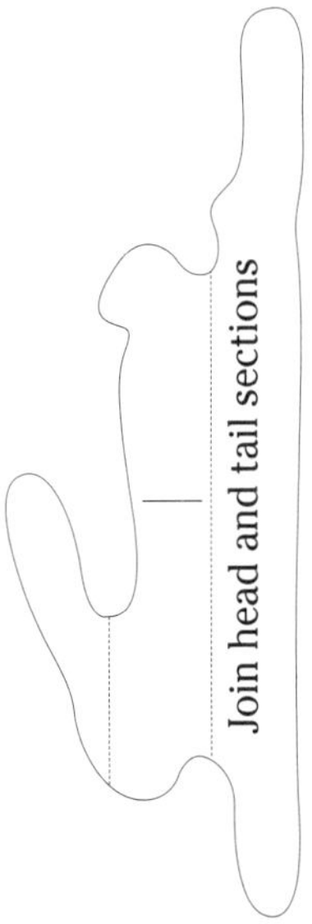

Join head and tail sections

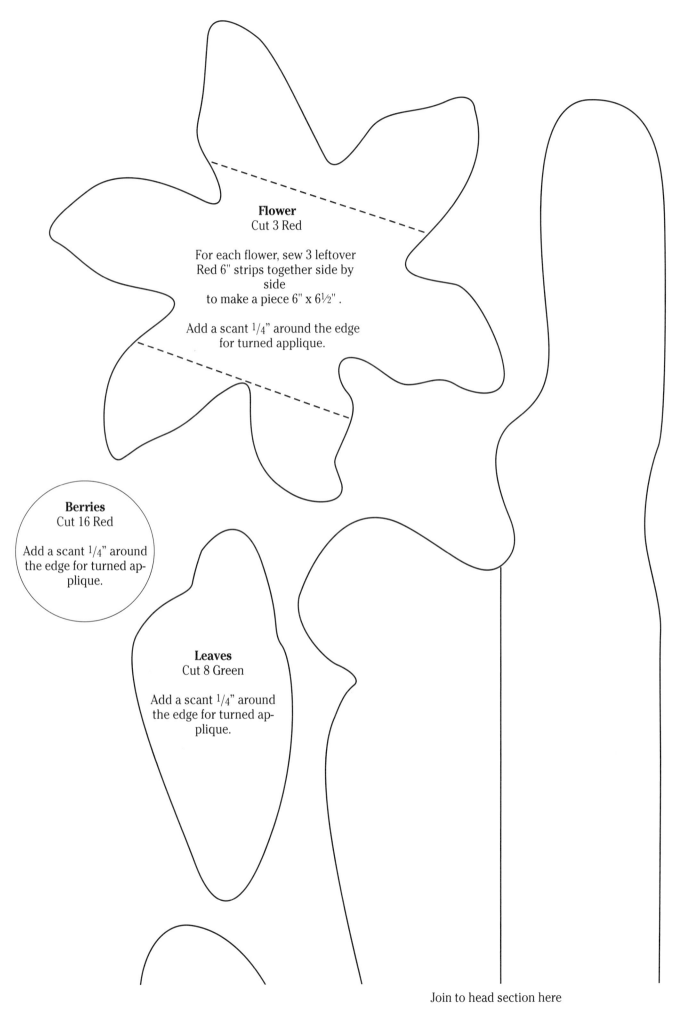

Flower
Cut 3 Red

For each flower, sew 3 leftover
Red 6" strips together side by
side
to make a piece 6" x 6½".

Add a scant $1/4$" around the edge
for turned applique.

Berries
Cut 16 Red

Add a scant $1/4$" around
the edge for turned ap-
plique.

Leaves
Cut 8 Green

Add a scant $1/4$" around
the edge for turned ap-
plique.

Join to head section here

Our Town

photo is on pages 10 - 11

SIZE: 60" x 74"
TIP: Add more borders to make a larger quilt.

YARDAGE:
Yardage is given for using either fabric yardage
    or 'Jelly Roll' strips.
We used a *Moda* "American Primer" by Minick & Simpson
    'Jelly Roll' collection of 2½" fabric strips
    - we purchased 1 'Jelly Roll'

14 strips	OR	1 yard White
5 strips	OR	⅜ yard Light Blue
4 strips	OR	⅓ yard Red
4 strips	OR	⅓ yard Navy
3 strips	OR	¼ yard Golden Brown
3 strips	OR	¼ yard Medium Blue
3 strips	OR	¼ yard Green
2 strips	OR	⅙ yard Border print

Border #2 & Binding	Purchase ⅞ yard Dark Blue
Border #3	Purchase 2¼ yards Medium Blue Border print
Backing	Purchase 3⅝ yards
Batting	Purchase 68" x 82"

Sewing machine, needle, thread

PREPARATION FOR STRIPS:
    Cut all strips 2½" by the width of fabric (usually 42" - 44").
    Label the stacks or pieces as you cut.

SORTING:
    Sort the following 2½" strips into stacks:

POSITION	QUANTITY & COLOR
Blocks 1, 3, 5, 9	4 Red
Blocks 1, 3, 4, 8, 9, 10	5 Light Blue
Blocks 1, 2, 3, 4, 6, 8, 9, 10	4 Navy
Blocks 2, 6, 7, 8 10	3 Golden Brown
Blocks 3, 5, 9, 10	3 Medium Blue
Blocks 2, 4, 6, 7, 8	3 Green
Blocks 1-10 and Border #1	14 White
Blocks 1, 5	2 Border prints

SEW BLOCKS:
    Refer to the Cutting Chart and Assembly instructions for each block.
    Label each piece as you cut.

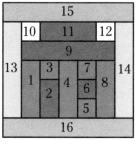

Block 3

BLOCK 3:
CUTTING CHART

Quantity	Length	Position
Red		
3	6½"	#1, 4, 8
3	2½"	#3, 5, 7
Navy		
1	10½"	# 9
1	6½"	#11
1	4½"	#2
1	2½"	#6
White		
2	2½"	#10, 12
Light Blue		
2	10½"	#13, 14
Medium Blue		
2	14½"	#15, 16

BLOCK 3 ASSEMBLY:
House:
    Column 1: #1
    Column 2: Sew 2-3. Press.
    Column 3: #4
    Column 4: Sew 5-6-7. Press.
    Column 5: #8
    Sew the columns together. Press.
Roof:
    Sew #9 to the top of the house. Press.
    Sew 10-11-12. Press.
    Sew 10-11-12 to the top of the house. Press.
Border: Sew #13 and 14 to the left and right sides
    of the block. Press.
    Sew #15 and 16 to the top and bottom of the
    block. Press.

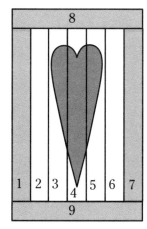

Block 5

BLOCK 5:
CUTTING CHART

Quantity	Length	Position
White		
5	18½"	#2, 3, 4, 5, 6
Medium Blue		
2	18½"	#1, 7
Border Print		
2	14½"	#8, 9
Red		
3	16½"	applique

BLOCK 5 ASSEMBLY:
Sew 1-2-3-4-5-6-7. Press.
Sew #8 and 9 to the top and bottom of the piece. Press.
Refer to the Finishing section of these instructions and
    applique the heart at this time if desired.

BLOCK 1:

CUTTING CHART

Quantity	Length	Position
Red		
3	10½"	#9, 11, 13
3	8½"	#1, 4, 8
3	5"	Window Unit
1	4½"	5
2	2½"	#3, 7
Navy		
1	10½"	#14
2	6½"	#2, 16
2	5"	Window Unit
2	2½"	#6, 19
Light Blue		
2	24½"	#21, 22
1	14½"	#23
White		
2	4½"	#18, 20
2	2½"	#15, 17
Border Print		
1	14½"	#24

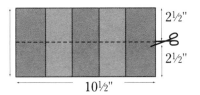

Window Units #10 & #12

Window Units:
> Sew Unit strips together Red-Navy-Red-Navy-Red to make a piece 5" x 10½".
> Cut the piece into 2 strips 2½" x 10½".
> Label 1 strip Unit 10 and the other Unit 12.

BLOCK 1 ASSEMBLY:
First Story:
> Column 1: #1
> Column 2: Sew 2-3. Press.
> Column 3: #4
> Column 4: Sew 5-6-7. Press.
> Column 5: #8
> Sew the columns together. Press.

Second Story:
> Refer to the Window Unit diagram to make Units #10 & #12.
> Sew #9-Unit 10-#11-Unit 12-#13. Press.
> Sew the Second Story to the House Section.

Roof: Sew #14 to the top of the house. Press.
> Sew #15-16-17. Press.
> Sew #18-19-20. Press.
> Sew the roof rows together. Press.
> Sew the roof to the house. Press.

Border: Sew #21 and 22 to the left and right sides of the block. Press.
> Sew #23 and 24 to the top and bottom of the block. Press.

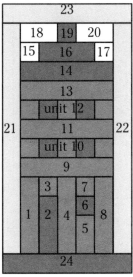

Block 1

BLOCK 2:

CUTTING CHART

Quantity	Length	Position
Navy		
1	5"	Center unit A
2	2½"	Center unit B & D
White		
2	5"	Center unit A
1	2½"	Center unit C
Green		
2	10½"	#3, 4
2	6½"	#1, 2
Brown		
2	14½"	#7, 8
2	10½"	#5, 6

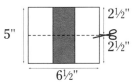

Center Unit

BLOCK 2 ASSEMBLY:
Checkerboard Center:
> Refer to the Center Unit diagram.
> Sew the Center Unit strips together White-Navy-White. to make a piece 5" x 6½". Press.
> Cut the piece into 2 units 2½" x 6½".
> Rows 1 & 3 are Unit A's.
> Row 2: Sew B-C-D. Press.
> Sew the rows together. Press.

Border:
> Sew #1 and 2 to the left and right sides of center. Press.
> Sew #3 and 4 to the top and bottom of the block. Press.
> Sew #5 and 6 to the left and right sides of the center. Press.
> Sew #7 and 8 to the top and bottom of the block. Press.

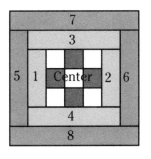

Block 2

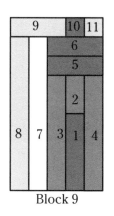

Block 9

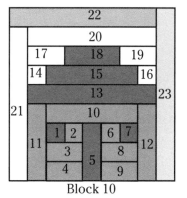

Block 10

BLOCK 10:

CUTTING CHART

Quantity	Length	Position
Navy		
1	14½"	#13
1	10½"	#15
2	6½"	#5, 18
2	2½"	#1, 7
Brown		
1	10½"	#10
2	8½"	#11, 12
4	4½"	#3, 4, 8, 9
2	2½"	#2, 6
White		
1	16½"	#21
1	14½"	#20
2	4½"	#17, 19
2	2½"	#14, 16
Medium Blue		
2	16½"	#22, 25
Light Blue		
1	18½"	#23

BLOCK 10 ASSEMBLY:

Sew 1-2. Press.
Sew 3 and 4 to the bottom. Press.
Sew #5 to the right side of the piece. Press.
Sew 6-7. Press.
Sew 8 and 9 to the bottom. Press.
Sew 6-7-8-9 to the right side of the block. Press.
Sew #10 to the top of the piece. Press.
Sew #11& 12 to the left and right side of the block. Press.
Sew #13 to the top of the block. Press.
Sew #14-15-16. Press.
Sew 14-15-16 to the top of the block. Press.
Sew 17-18-19. Press.
Sew 17-18-19 to the top of the block. Press.
Sew #20 to the top of the block. Press.
Sew #21 to the left side of the block. Press.
Sew #22 to the top of the block. Press.
Sew #23 to the right side of the block. Press.
Sew Block 9 to Block 10. Press.
Sew 24-25. Press.
Sew 24-25 to the bottom of the block. Press.

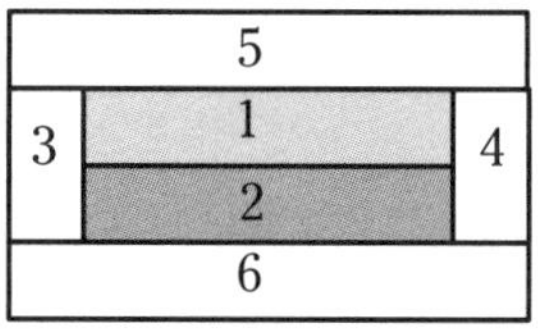

BLOCK 9:

CUTTING CHART

Quantity	Length	Position
Red		
2	12½"	#3, 4
1	4½"	#2
Navy		
1	8½"	#1
2	6½"	#5, 6
1	2½"	#10
Light Blue		
1	16½"	#8
1	6½"	#9
1	2½"	#11
White		
1	16½"	#7
Medium Blue		
1	12½"	#24

BLOCK 9 ASSEMBLY:

Sew 1- 2. Press.
Sew #3 to the left side of the block. Press.
Sew #4 to the right side of the block. Press.
Sew #5 & 6 to the top of the block. Press.
Sew #7 & 8 to the left side of the block. Press.
Sew #9-10-11. Press.
Sew 9-10-11 to the top of the block. Press.
Note:
You will use #24 after you sew Blocks 9 and 10 together.

BLOCK 7:

CUTTING CHART

Quantity	Length	Position
Brown		
1	10½"	#1
Green		
1	10½"	#2
White		
2	14½"	#5, 6
2	4½"	#3, 4

BLOCK 7 ASSEMBLY:

Sew #1 and 2. Press.
Sew #3 and 4 to the right and left sides of the block. Press.
Sew #5 and 6 to the top and bottom of the block. Press.

Block 7

BLOCK 4:

CUTTING CHART

Quantity	Length	Position
Light Blue		
2	18"	Unit #1
Navy		
1	2½"	#5
Green		
4	4½"	#2, 3, 4, 6
White		
2	14½"	#9, 10
2	10½"	#7, 8

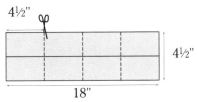

Unit #1 for Block 4

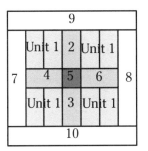

Block 4

BLOCK 4 ASSEMBLY:

Unit 1: Refer to the Unit 1 diagram.
Sew 2 Light Blue strips together to make a piece 4½" x 18".
Cut the piece into 4 units 4½" x 4½".
Rows 1 & 3: Sew Unit 1-#2-Unit 1. Press. Make 2.
Row 2: Sew 4-5-6. Press.
Sew the rows together. Press.
Sew #7 and 8 to the left and right sides of the block. Press.
Sew #9 and 10 to the top and bottom of the block. Press.

BLOCK 6:

CUTTING CHART

Quantity	Length	Position
Navy		
2	6½"	#1, 3
Brown		
1	6½"	#2
Green		
2	10½"	#6, 7
2	6½"	#4, 5
White		
2	14½"	#10, 11
2	10½"	#8, 9

BLOCK 6 ASSEMBLY:

Sew 1- 2-3. Press.
Sew #4 and 5 to the right and left sides of the block. Press.
Sew #6 and 7 to the top and bottom of the block. Press.
Sew #8 and 9 to the right and left sides of the block. Press.
Sew #10 and 11 to the top and bottom of the block. Press.

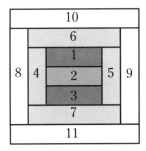

Block 6

BLOCK 8:

CUTTING CHART

Quantity	Length	Position
Navy		
1	2½"	#2
Brown		
1	6½"	#5
1	4½"	#4
Green		
1	10½"	#9
1	8½"	#8
White		
1	8½"	7
1	6½"	6
1	4½"	3
1	2½"	1
Light Blue		
2	14½"	#12, 13
2	10½"	#10, 11

BLOCK 8 ASSEMBLY:

Sew 1- 2. Press.
Sew #3 to the right side of the block. Press.
Sew #4 to the bottom of the block. Press.
Sew #5 left side of the block. Press.
Sew #6 to the top of the block. Press.
Sew #7 to the right side of the block. Press.
Sew #8 to the bottom of the block. Press.
Sew #9 and 10 to the left side of the block. Press.
Sew #11 to the right side of the block. Press.
Sew #12 & 13 to the top and bottom of the block. Press.

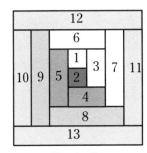

Block 8

ASSEMBLY:
>   Arrange all blocks on a work
>   surface or table.
>   Refer to diagram for block
>   placement and direction.

Section 1:
>   Sew Block 6 to the bottom of Block 1. Press.
>   Sew Block 8 to the bottom of Block 6. Press.

Section 2:
>   Sew Block 2 to the left side of Block 3. Press.
>   Sew Block 7 to the bottom of Block 4. Press.
>   Sew Block 4-7 to the left side of Block 5. Press.

Assemble the Top of Section 2:
>   Sew Block 4-5-7 to the bottom of Block 2-3. Press.

Assemble the Bottom of Section 2:
>   Sew Block 9-10 to the bottom of Section 2. Press.
>   Sew Section 1 to the left side of Section 2. Press.

Section 1	**Section 2**	
Block 1	Block 2	Block 3
Block 6	Block 4	Block 5
Block 8	Block 7	
	Block 9-10	

Heart
Cut 1 Red 16½" long
Cut 2 Red 14½" long

Sew 3 Red strips together to make a
piece 6½" x 16½" for the heart.

Add a scant ¼" around the edge for
turned applique.

Join to bottom of heart here

RDERS:

ced Border #1:

5 White strips together end to end.
  Cut 2 strips 2½" x 56½" for sides.
  Cut 2 strips 2½" x 46½" for top and bottom.
  Sew side borders to the quilt. Press.
  Sew top and bottom borders to the quilt. Press.

er Border #2:

strips 2½" by the width of fabric.
strips together end to end.
  Cut 2 strips 2½" x 60½" for sides.
  Cut 2 strips 2½" x 50½" for top and bottom.
  Sew side borders to the quilt. Press.
  Sew top and bottom borders to the quilt. Press.

ered Border #3:

er to the Mitered Border instructions on page 21.
 border print was 5" wide so we cut our strips 5½" wide.
  Cut 2 strips 5½" x 80½" for sides.
  Cut 2 strips 5½" x 66½" for top and bottom.
  Sew side borders to the quilt. Press.
  Sew top and bottom borders to the quilt. Press.
  Miter (see page 21) the corners. Press.

ISHING:

plique:
  See Basic Instructions.
  You will need to sew 3 Red strips together to make a
      piece 6½" x 16½" before cutting the heart pattern.
  Cut out pieces using patterns. Applique as desired.

ilting:
  See Basic Instructions.

ding:
  Cut strips 2½" wide.
  Sew together end to end to equal 278".
  See Binding Instructions.

Our Town
Quilt Assembly Diagram

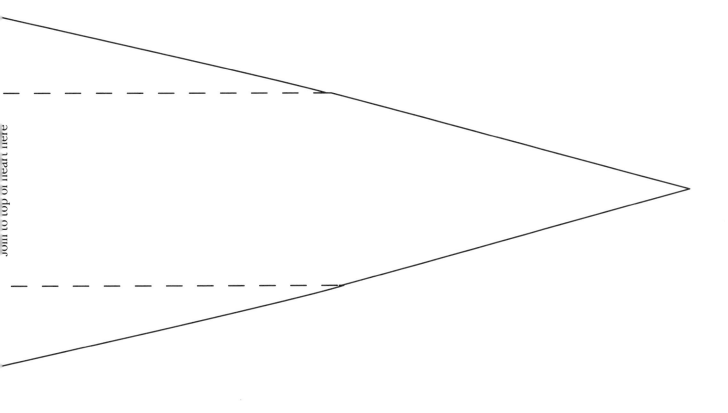

Join to top of heart here

Hometown Houses

photo is on page 12

SIZE: 66" x 86"
TIP: Add more borders to make a larger quilt.

YARDAGE:
Yardage is given for using either fabric yardage or
    'Jelly Roll' strips.
We used a *Moda* "Wildflower Serenade"
    by Kansas Troubles
    'Jelly Roll' collection of 2½" fabric strips
    - we purchased 1 'Jelly Roll'

6 strips	OR	½ yard Black
5 strips	OR	⅜ yard Dark Blue
5 strips	OR	⅜ yard Tan
5 strips	OR	⅜ yard Green
5 strips	OR	⅜ yard Red
4 strips	OR	⅓ yard Medium Blue
4 strips	OR	⅓ yard Brown

Sky Background	Purchase ¾ yd Tan solid
Border #3	Purchase ½ yd Red
Border #4 & Binding	Purchase 2⅛ yds Black
Backing	Purchase 5⅓ yards
Batting	Purchase 74" x 94"
Sewing machine, needle, thread	

PREPARATION FOR STRIPS:
    Cut all strips 2½" by the width of fabric
        (usually 42" - 44").
    Label the stacks or pieces as you cut.

SORTING:
    Sort the following 2½" strips into stacks:

POSITION	QUANTITY & COLOR
Roofs, doors, windows:	6 Black
Houses C, E, F:	5 Dark Blue
Houses D, F, I:	4 Brown
Houses A & H, Sashes:	5 Green
Houses B, G, J, & Sash corners:	5 Red
House F, I & Border #1:	5 Tan
Border #2:	4 Med. Blue

SEW BLOCKS:
    Refer to the Cutting Chart and Assembly
        instructions for each block.
    Label the pieces as you cut.

SECTION CONSTRUCTION:
Refer to the Quilt Assembly diagram.
Arrange all blocks on a work surface or table.

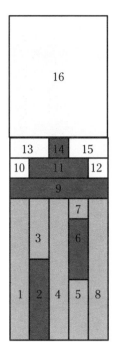

House A

HOUSE A:

CUTTING CHART

Quantity	Length	Position
Tan yardage		
1	10½" x 12½"	#16
2	2½" x 4½"	#13, 15
2	2½" x 2½"	#10, 12
Black		
1	10½"	#9
1	8½	#2
2	6½"	#6, 11
1	2½"	#14
Green		
3	14½"	#1, 4, 8
2	6½"	#3, 5
1	2½"	#7

HOUSE A ASSEMBLY:
Refer to the House A diagram.
House section: Sew #2-#3. Press.
    Sew #1 and #4 on the right and
        left sides of the piece.
        Press.
    Sew 5-6-7. Press.
    Sew to piece 1-4. Press.
    Sew #8 to the right side of the
        piece. Press.
Roof section:
    Sew 10-11-12. Press.
    Sew 9 to the bottom of 10-11-12
        piece. Press.
    Sew 13-14-15. Press.
    Sew 13-14-15 to the top of the
        piece. Press.
    Sew #16 to the top of the roof.
        Press.
    Sew the House and Roof
        sections together. Press.

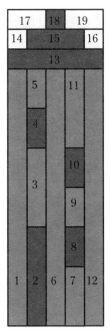

House B

HOUSE B:

CUTTING CHART

Quantity	Length	Position
Tan yardage		
2	2½" x 4½"	#17, 19
2	2½" x 2½"	#14, 16
Red		
3	26½"	#1, 6, 12
2	8½"	#3, 11
1	6½"	#7
2	4½"	#5, 9
Black		
2	10½"	#2, 13
1	6½"	#15
3	4½"	#4, 8, 10
1	2½"	#18

HOUSE B ASSEMBLY:
Refer to the House B diagram.
House section:
    Sew 2-3-4-5. Press.
    Sew #1 & #6 to the left and
        right sides of
        the piece. Press.
    Sew 7-8-9-10-11. Press.
    Sew to the right side of the
        piece. Press.
    Sew #12 to the right side of
        the piece. Press.
Roof section:
    Sew #13 to the top of the
        house section.
    Sew 14-15-16. Press.
    Sew 17-18-19. Press.
    Sew the roof strips to the
        house. Press.

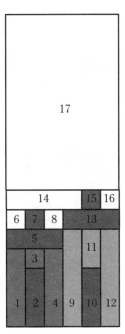

House C-D

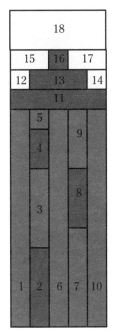

House E

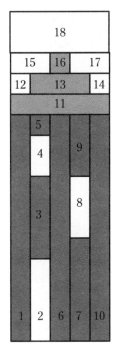

House F

HOUSE C–D:

CUTTING CHART

Quantity	Length	Position
Tan yardage		
1	12½" x 18½"	#17
1	2½" x 8½"	#14
3	2½" x 2½"	#6, 8, 16
Dark Blue		
2	8½"	#1, 4
1	2½"	#3
Black		
4	6½"	#2, 5, 10, 13
2	2½"	#7, 15
Brown		
2	10½"	#9 , 12
1	4½"	#11

HOUSE C & D ASSEMBLY:
Refer to the House C-D diagram.
House C: Sew #2-3. Press.
  Sew #1 & #4 to the left and right
    sides of the piece. Press.
  Sew #5 to the top of the piece.
  Sew #6-7-8. Press.
  Sew to the top of the piece.
    Press.
  House C is now complete.
House D: Sew #10-11. Press.
  Sew #9 & #12 to the left and right
    sides of the piece. Press.
  Sew #13 to the top of the piece.
  Sew House C to House D. Press.
  Sew #14-15-16. Press.
  Sew to the top of the piece.
    Press.
  Sew #17 to the top of the piece.
    Press.

HOUSE E:

CUTTING CHART

Quantity	Length	Position
Tan yardage		
1	4½" x 10½"	#18
2	2½" x 4½"	#15, 17
2	2½" x 2½"	#12, 14
Dark Blue		
3	22½"	#1, 6, 10
1	10½"	#7
1	8½"	#3
1	6½"	#9
1	2½"	#5
Black		
1	10½"	#11
1	8½"	#2
2	6½"	#8, 13
1	4½"	#4
1	2½"	#16

HOUSE E ASSEMBLY:
Refer to the House E diagram.
House section: Sew #2-3-4-5. Press.
  Sew #1 & #6 to the left and right
    sides of the piece. Press.
  Sew #7-8-9. Press.
  Sew to the right side of the piece.
    Press.
  Sew #10 to the right side of the
    piece. Press.
Roof section: Sew #11 to the top of
the house. Press.
  Sew #12-13-14. Press.
  Sew to the top of the house. Press.
  Sew 15-16-17. Press.
  Sew to the top of the house. Press.
  Sew #18 to the top of the house.
    Press.

HOUSE F:

CUTTING CHART

Quantity	Length	Position
Tan yardage		
1	4½" x 10½"	#18.
2	2½" x 4½"	#15, 17
2	2½" x 2½"	#12, 14
Dark Blue		
3	22½"	#1, 6, 10
1	10½"	#7
1	8½"	#3
1	6½"	#9
1	2½"	#5
Brown		
1	10½"	#11
1	6½"	#13
1	2½"	#16
Tan strips		
1	8½"	#2
1	6½"	#8
1	4½"	#4

HOUSE F ASSEMBLY:
  Refer to the House F diagram.
  Follow the instructions for
    House E.

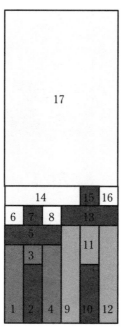

House G-H

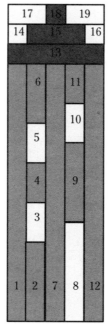

House I

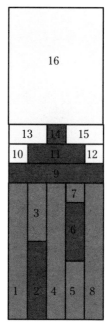

House J

HOUSE G–H:

CUTTING CHART

Quantity	Length	Position
Tan yardage		
1	12½" x 18½"	#17
1	2½" x 8½"	#14
3	2½" x 2½"	#6, 8, 16
Red		
2	8½"	#1, 4
1	2½"	#3
Black		
4	6½"	#2, 5, 10, 13
2	2½"	#7, 15
Green		
2	10½"	#9, 12
1	4½"	#11

HOUSE G & H ASSEMBLY:
Refer to the House G-H
diagram.
Follow the instructions
for Houses C-D.

HOUSE I:

CUTTING CHART

Quantity	Length	Position
Tan yardage		
2	2½" x 4½"	#17, 19
2	2½" x 2½"	#14, 16
Brown		
3	26½"	#1, 7, 12
2	8½"	#2, 9
1	6½"	#6
2	4½"	#4, 11
Black		
1	10½"	#13
1	6½"	#15
1	2½"	#18
Tan		
1	10½"	#8
3	4½"	#3, 5, 10

HOUSE I ASSEMBLY:
Refer to the House I diagram.
House section: Sew #2-3-4-5-6.
Press.
Sew #1 & #7 to the left and
right sides of the piece.
Press.
Sew #8-9-10-11. Press.
Sew to the right side of the
piece. Press.
Sew #12 to the right side of the
piece. Press.

Roof section: Sew #13 to the top of
the piece. Press.
Sew 14-15-16. Press.
Sew 17-18-19. Press.
Sew the roof strips to the
house. Press.

HOUSE J:

CUTTING CHART

Quantity	Length	Position
Tan yardage		
1	10½" x 12½"	#16
2	2½" x 4½"	#13, 15
2	2½" x 2½"	#10, 12
Black		
1	10½"	#9
1	8½"	#2
2	6½"	#6, 11
1	2½"	#14
Red		
3	14½	#1, 4, 8
2	6½"	#3, 5
1	2½"	#7

HOUSE J ASSEMBLY:
Refer to the House J
diagram.
Follow the instructions
for House A.

SASHINGS:
   Cut 3 Green strips 2½" x 42½".
   Cut 6 Red squares 2½" x 2½".
   Sew a Red square to each end of each sashing. Press.

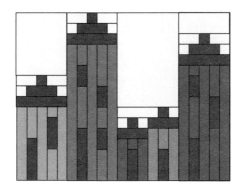

Section 1: Sew Houses A-B-C-D-E. Press.
Side Borders #1:
   Sew Tan strips end to end. Press.
   Cut 4 strips 32½" long.
   Sew a Tan side border strip to the right and left
      sides of Section 1. Press.
   Sew a Sashing strip to the top and bottom of Sec-
tion 1. Press.

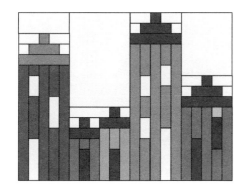

Section 2: Sew Houses F-G-H-I-J. Press.
   Sew a Tan side border strip to the right and left
      sides of Section 2. Press.
   Sew a Sashing strip to the bottom of Section 2. Press.

ASSEMBLY:
   Sew Section 1 to Section 2. Press.

BORDERS:
Medium Blue Side Border #2:
You need 4 strips
Sew 2 strips together end to end.
Repeat for remaining 2 strips.
   Cut 2 strips 2½" x 70½" .
   Sew side borders to the quilt. Press.

Border #3:
Cut strips 2½" by the width of fabric.
Sew strips together end to end.
   Cut 2 strips 2½" x 70½" for sides.
   Cut 2 strips 2½" x 54½" for top and bottom.
   Sew side borders to the quilt. Press.
   Sew top and bottom borders to the quilt. Press.

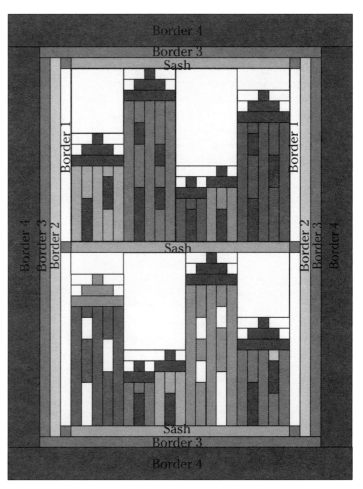

Hometown Houses - Assembly Diagram

Outer Border #4:
Cut strips 6½" wide parallel to the selvage to
      eliminate piecing.
   Cut 2 strips 6½" x 74½" for sides.
   Cut 2 strips 6½" x 66½" for top and bottom.
   Sew side borders to the quilt. Press.
   Sew top and bottom borders to the quilt. Press.

FINISHING:
Quilting: See Basic Instructions.
Binding: Cut strips 2½" wide.
         Sew together end to end to equal 314".
         See Binding Instructions.

Favorite Things

photo is on page 13

SIZE: 50" x 62"
TIP: Add more borders to make a larger quilt.

YARDAGE:
Yardage is given for using either fabric yardage or
    'Jelly Roll' strips.
We used a *Moda* "Recess" by American Jane
'Jelly Roll' collection of 2½" fabric strips
- we purchased 1 'Jelly Roll'

6 strips	OR	½ yard Blue
6 strips	OR	½ yard Yellow
5 strips	OR	⅜ yard Green
5 strips	OR	⅜ yard Red
4 strips	OR	⅓ yard Orange
4 strips	OR	⅓ yard Navy
3 strips	OR	¼ yard Ivory

Border #1	Purchase ⅜ yard Navy
Border #2 & Binding	Purchase 1⅝ yards Red
Backing	Purchase 2⅞ yards
Batting	Purchase 58" x 70"

Sewing machine, needle, thread
4 Black ¼" buttons for eyes on the cat, dog, and bird
DMC Black pearl cotton or 6-ply floss
#22 or #24 chenille needle

PREPARATION FOR STRIPS:
    Cut all strips 2½" by the width of fabric
        (usually 42" - 44").
    Label the stacks or pieces as you cut.

SORTING:
    Sort the 2½" strips into stacks according
        to color and length.

MAKING THE BLOCKS:
    Refer to the Cutting Chart for each block.

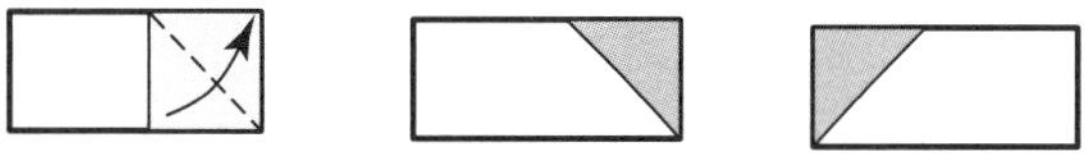

Snowball Corner Diagram

SNOWBALL CORNERS:
    Some strips in the blocks use the Snowball Cor-
ner technique. The direction of the diagonal for each
strip in the block varies, so you must carefully note
the diagonal on the block assembly diagram. Some
strips have a corner on only one end. The squares
used as Snowball Corners are labelled with a "c" in
the cutting list.
    Tip: Fold back the triangle and check its position
before you sew.
    Align a square with the appropriate end of the
strip and sew on the diagonal line. Fold the triangle
back and press before attaching it to any other strips.

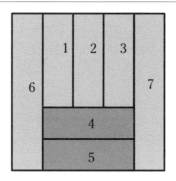

Flower Pot

FLOWER POT BLOCK A

CUTTING CHART

	Quantity	Length	Position
Green	2	10½"	#6, 7
	3	6½"	#1, 2, 3
Orange	2	6½"	#4, 5
Navy	1	8"	Applique
Red	1	7½"	Applique

ASSEMBLY:
    Sew 1-2-3. Press.
    Sew 4-5. Press.
    Sew 1-2-3 to 4-5. Press.
    Sew #6 and 7 to the left and right sides of the piece. Press.
    Refer to the Finishing section for Applique instructions.
    Applique the flowers and leaves at this time if desired.

Flower
Cut 3 Red for A

Add a scant ¼" seam al-
lowance before
cutting.

Leaf
Cut 3 Navy for A

Add a scant ¼" seam
allowance before
cutting.

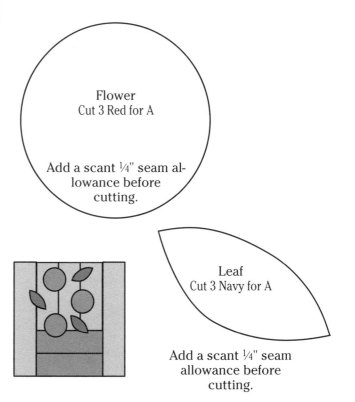

TREE
BLOCK B

CUTTING CHART

	Quantity	Length	Position
Green	3	6½"	#1, 2, 3
Yellow	2	10½"	#7, 8
	2	4½"	#4, 6
	4	2½"	#1c, 1c, 3c, 3c
Navy	1	4½"	#5

ASSEMBLY:
   Align 2 Snowball Corner squares
      on #1. Align 2 squares on #3.

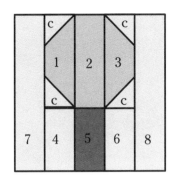

Tree

Refer to the Snowball Corner instructions.
Sew on the diagonals, fold back the pieces and press.
Sew 1-2-3. Press.
Sew 4-5-6. Press.
Sew 1-2-3 to 4-5-6. Press.
   Sew #7 and 8 to the left and right
      sides of the piece. Press.

CAT
BLOCK C

CUTTING CHART

	Quantity	Length	Position
Blue	5	4½"	#5, 6, 9, 10, 11
	3	2½"	#2, 7c, 7c
Yellow	1	10½"	#7
	1	6½"	#4
	2	4½"	#8, 12
	4	2½"	#1, 3, 10c, 10c
	1	1½" x 1½"	#9c

ASSEMBLY:
   Align 2 Snowball squares on #7.
   Align 2 Snowball squares on #10.
   Align 1 small Snowball square on #9.

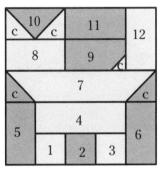

Cat

Refer to the Snowball Corner instructions.
Sew on the diagonal, fold back pieces and press.
Sew 1-2-3. Press.
Sew #4 to the top of 1-2-3. Press.
Sew 5 and 6 to the left and right sides of unit. Press.
Sew #7 to the top of the piece. Press.
Sew 8-9. Press.
Sew 10-11. Press.
Sew 8-9 to 10-11. Press.
Sew 12 to the right side of the 8-9-10-11. Press.
Sew 8-9-10-11-12 to the top of the piece. Press.

HOUSE – BLOCK D

CUTTING CHART

	Quantity	Length	Position
Blue	6	2½"	#8c, 8c, 9c, 9c, 10, 11
Navy	1	10½"	#8
	1	6½"	#9
	1	4½"	#5
	1	2½"	#1
Orange	1	10½"	#7
	3	4½"	#3, 4, 6
	1	2½"	#2

ASSEMBLY:
   Align 2 Snowball squares on #8.
   Align 2 Snowball squares on #9.
   Refer to Snowball Corner instructions.
   Sew on the diagonal, fold back pieces
      and press.
   Sew 1-2. Press.
   Sew #3 to the left side of 1-2. Press.
   Sew 4-5-6. Press.
   Sew 4-5-6 to the right side of 1-2-3.
      Press.
   Sew 9-10-11. Press. Sew 7-8-9. Press.
   Sew 7-8-9 to the top of the piece. Press.

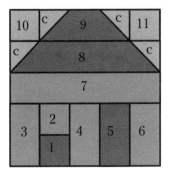

House

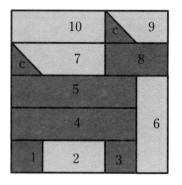

SCOTTY DOG BLOCK E

CUTTING CHART

	Quantity	Length	Position
Navy	2	8½"	#4, 5
	1	4½"	#8
	4	2½"	#1, 3, 7c, 9c
Green	3	6½"	#6, 7, 10
	2	4½"	#2, 9

Scotty Dog

ASSEMBLY:
Align 1 Snowball Corner square on #7.
Align 1 Snowball Corner square on #9.
Refer to the Snowball Corner instructions.
Sew on the diagonal, fold back the pieces and press.
Sew 1-2-3. Press.
Sew 4-5. Press.
Sew 4-5 to the top of 1-2-3. Press.
Sew #6 to the right side of the piece. Press.
Sew 7-8. Press.
Sew 9-10. Press.
Sew 7-8 and 9-10 to the top of the piece. Press.

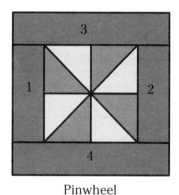

Pinwheel

PINWHEEL BLOCK F

CUTTING CHART

	Quantity	Length	Position
Orange	2	9"	Pinwheel
Yellow	2	9"	Pinwheel
Navy	1	2½"	Applique
Red	2	10½"	#3, 4
	2	6½"	#1, 2

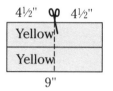
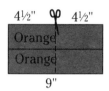

MAKE SQUARES FOR PINWHEELS:
Sew 2 Orange strips together to make a piece 4½" x 9".
Cut piece into 2 squares 4½" x 4½".
Repeat for the Yellow strips.

HALF-SQUARE TRIANGLES:
Pair up 2 sets of Orange and Yellow squares.
Follow the instructions in the Half-Square Triangle Diagram on page 75.
Make 4 half-square triangles.
Center and trim each square to 3½" x 3½".

Pinwheel Assembly

PINWHEEL:
Arrange the half-square triangles as shown in the Pinwheel diagram with 2 rows, 2 squares per row.
Sew the squares together. Press.
Sew the rows together. Press.

ASSEMBLY:
Sew strips #1 and #2 to the left and right of the pinwheel. Press.
Sew strips #3 and #4 to the top and bottom of the piece. Press.
Cut out a Navy circle and applique it to the center of the pinwheel.

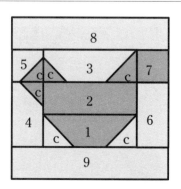

Bird

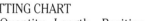

BIRD – BLOCK G

CUTTING CHART

	Quantity	Length	Position
Blue	2	6½"	#1, 2
	2	2½"	#3c, 7
	3	2" x 2"	#3c, 4c, 5c
Yellow	2	10½	#8, 9
	1	6½"	#3
	2	4½"	#4, 6
	3	2½"	#1c, 1c, 5

ASSEMBLY:
Align 1 Snowball squares on #5.
Align 1 Snowball square on #4.
Align 2 Snowball squares on #1.
Align 2 Snowball squares on #3 (the 2" square #3c is on the left end of #3).
Refer to Snowball Corner instructions.
Sew on the diagonal, fold back the pieces and press.
Sew 1-2-3. Press.
Sew 4-5. Press.
Sew 6-7. Press.
Sew 4-5 to the left of 1-2-3. Press.
Sew 6-7 to the right of 1-2-3. Press.
Sew 8 and 9 to the top and bottom of piece. Press.

SMALL HEART
BLOCK H

CUTTING CHART

Quantity	Length	Position
Blue		
1	10½"	#9
2	6½"	#7, 8
2	5½"	#1, 2
2	2½"	#3c, 3c
4	1½"x 1½"	#5c, 5c, 6c, 6c
Red		
2	6½"	#3, 4
2	3½"	#5, 6
2	1½"x 1½"	#1c, 2c

ASSEMBLY:

Align 1 Snowball square on #1.
Align 1 Snowball square on #2.
Align 2 Snowball squares on #3
Align 2 Snowball squares on #5
Align 2 Snowball squares on #6.
Refer to Snowball Corner instructions.
Sew on the diagonal, fold back pieces, press.
Sew 1-2. Press.
Sew 5-6. Press.
Sew 3-4-5/6. Press.
Sew strips #7 and #8 to the left and right sides of piece. Press.
Sew strip #9 to the top of the piece. Press.
Sew 1-2 to the bottom of the piece. Press.

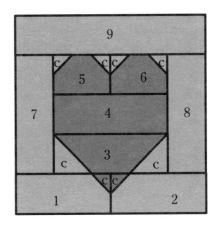

Small Heart

FLOWER BASKET
BLOCK I

CUTTING CHART

Quantity	Length	Position
Blue	1	10½"	#5
	2	6½"	#1, 2
Yellow	2	10½"	#6, 7
	2	4½"	#3, 4
	6	2½"	#1c, 1c, 2c, 2c, 5c, 5c
Navy	1	8"	Applique
Red	1	7½"	Applique

ASSEMBLY:

Align 2 Snowball squares on #1.
Align 2 Snowball squares on #2.
Align 2 Snowball squares on # 5.
Refer to Snowball Corner instructions.
Sew on the diagonal, fold back pieces and press.
Sew 1-2. Press.
Sew strips #3 and 4 to the left and right sides of the piece. Press.
Sew #5-6-7 to the top of the piece. Press.
Refer to Applique instructions.
Applique flowers and leaves at this time if desired.

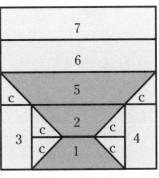

Flower Basket

Flower
Cut 3 Red for I

Add a scant ¼" seam allowance before cutting.

Leaf
Cut 3 Navy for I

Add a scant ¼" seam allowance before cutting.

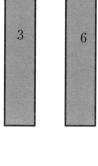

BUTTERFLY BLOCK J

CUTTING CHART

	Quantity	Length	Position
Green	7	2½"	#5, "c"
Orange	2	10½"	#3, 6
	2	8½"	#2, 7
	2	2½"x 3"	#1, 8
Navy	1	8½"	#4
	1	13"	Applique

ASSEMBLY:

Align 1 Snowball square on #2
Align 1 Snowball square on #7.
Align 1 Snowball square on #3.
Align 1 Snowball square on #6.
TIP: Aligning a Snowball square on the
   end of #1 and #8 may seem a little
   tricky. Simply align it along the
   edge, notice the direction of the
   diagonal, and sew it in place.
   (Do not sew two 2½"x 2½" squares
   to make half square triangles or
   they will turn out too small.)
Align 1 Snowball square on #1.
Align 1 Snowball square on #8.
Refer to Snowball Corner instructions.
Sew on the diagonal, fold back pieces
   and press.
Sew 1-2. Press.
Sew 4-5. Press.
Sew 7-8. Press.
Sew the columns together. Press.
Refer to Applique instructions.
Applique wing pieces in place at
   this time if desired.
Since the antennae extend beyond the
   block, embroidery is done after
   blocks are assembled.

Butterfly

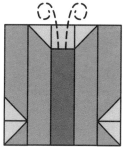

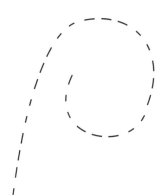

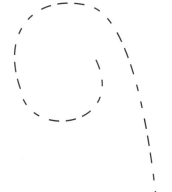

Add a scant ¼"
seam allowance
before
cutting for turned
edge applique.

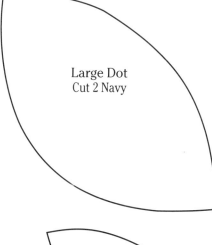

Large Dot
Cut 2 Navy

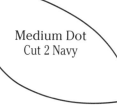

Medium Dot
Cut 2 Navy

Running Stitch

Small Dot
Cut 2 Navy

TALL HEART BLOCK K

CUTTING CHART

	Quantity	Length	Position
Ivory	5	22½"	#1, 2, 3, 4, 5
Red	3	16½"	Heart applique

ASSEMBLY:

Sew 5 Ivory strips together side by side to make a piece 10½" x 22½". Press.

Sew 3 Red strips together side by side to make a piece 6½" x 16½". Press.

Refer to Applique instructions. Applique the heart at this time if desired.

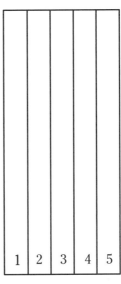

1 2 3 4 5

Tall Heart

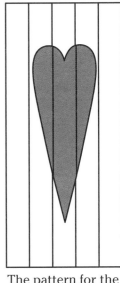

The pattern for the heart applique is on pages 44 - 45.

SASHING STRIPS

CUTTING CHART for SASHING STRIPS:

	Quantity	Length	Position of Sashing
Orange	4	10½"	A, L, T, W
Red	7	10½"	B, D, G, I, K, Q, BB
Blue	8	10½"	C, E, N, P, V, Y, AA, DD
Green	8	10½"	F, H, M, O, R, U, X, CC
Yellow	3	10½"	J, S, Z
Navy	20	2½"	Cornerstones - C

C	Sashing E	C	Sashing F	C	Sashing G	C

Horizontal Sashing #1

C	Sashing H	C	Sashing I	C	Sashing J	C

Horizontal Sashing #2

C	Sashing T	C	Sashing U	C	Sashing W	C

Horizontal Sashing #3

C	Sashing X	C	Sashing Y	C	Sashing Z	C

Horizontal Sashing #4

ASSEMBLY:

Arrange all blocks on a work surface or table.

Refer to diagram for block placement and direction.

Horizontal Sashing:

Sew and press each combination listed below.

Sashing #1: C - Sashing E - C - Sashing F - C - Sashing G - C

Sashing #2: C - Sashing H - C - Sashing I - C - Sashing J - C

Sashing #3: C - Sashing T - C - Sashing U - C - Sashing W - C

Sashing #4: C - Sashing X - C - Sashing Y - C - Sashing Z - C

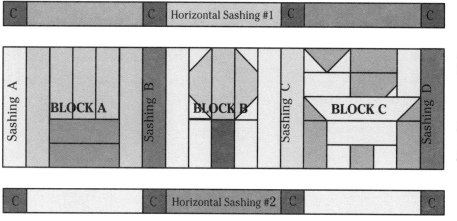

Assemble Section A:
Sew Sashing A - Block A -
   Sashing B - Block B -
   Sashing C- Block C-
   Sashing D. Press.
Sew Horizontal Sashing #1 to the
   top of the section. Press.
Sew Horizontal Sashing #2 to the
   bottom of the section. Press.

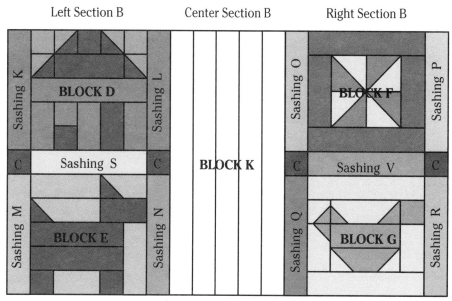

Assemble Section B:
Sew Sashing K - C - Sashing M. Press.
Sew Sashing L - C - Sashing N. Press.
Sew Sashing O - C - Sashing Q. Press.
Sew Sashing P - C - Sashing R. Press.

Sew Block D - Sashing S - Block E. Press.
Sew Block F - Sashing V - Block G. Press.

Left Section B:
Sew K - C - M to the left of D - S - E. Press.
Sew L - C - N to the right of D - S - E. Press.

Right Section B:
Sew O - C - Q to the left of F - V - G. Press.
Sew P - C - R to the right of F - V - G. Press.

Left, Center and Right Section B:
Sew the Left Section B to the left
   of Block K.
Sew the Right Section B to the right
   of Block K.

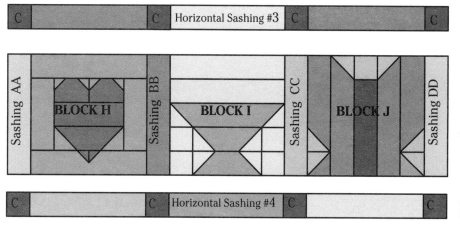

Assemble Section C:
Sew Sashing AA - Block H -
   Sashing BB - Block I -
   Sashing CC- Block J -
   Sashing DD. Press.
Sew Horizontal Sashing #3 to the
   top of the row. Press.
Sew Horizontal Sashing #4 to the
   bottom of the row. Press.

Assemble the Center of the Quilt:
Sew Section A to the top of Section B.
   Press.
Sew Section C to the bottom of Section B.
   Press.

Favorite Things
Section Assembly Diagram

Favorite Things - Quilt Assembly Diagram

BORDERS:

Border #1:
Cut strips 2½" by the width of fabric.
Sew strips together end to end.
> Cut 2 strips 2½" x 50½" for sides.
> Cut 2 strips 2½" x 42½" for top and bottom.
> Sew side borders to the quilt. Press.
> Sew top and bottom borders to the quilt. Press.

Border #2:
Cut strips 4½" wide parallel to the selvage to eliminate piecing.
> Cut 2 strips 4½" x 54½" for sides.
> Cut 2 strips 4½" x 50½" for top and bottom.
> Sew side borders to the quilt. Press.
> Sew top and bottom borders to the quilt. Press.

FINISHING:

Applique:
> See Basic Instructions.
> Cut out pieces from patterns. Applique as desired.

Quilting:
> See Basic Instructions.

Binding:
> Cut strips 2½" wide.
> Sew together end to end to equal 234".
> See Binding Instructions.

> Embroider the butterfly antennae with a long and short Running stitch.
> Sew a button for the eye on the cat, dog, and bird, and stitch a button for the dog's nose.

Home Garden

photo is on page 14

SIZE: 42" x 58"
TIP: Add more borders to make a larger quilt.

YARDAGE:
Yardage is given for using either fabric yardage or
'Jelly Roll' strips.
We used a *Moda* "Butterfly Fling" by Me & My Sister
'Jelly Roll' collection of 2½" fabric strips
- we purchased 1 'Jelly Roll'

7 strips	OR	½ yard White
6 strips	OR	½ yard Purple
4 strips	OR	⅓ yard Pink
4 strips	OR	⅓ yard Green
4 strips	OR	⅓ yard Blue
2 strips	OR	⅙ yard Yellow

Border & Binding	Purchase 1½ yards Green
Backing	Purchase 2⅓ yards
Batting	Purchase 50" x 66"
Sewing machine, needle, thread	

PREPARATION FOR STRIPS:
Cut all strips 2½" by the width of fabric
(usually 42" - 44").
Label the stacks or pieces as you cut.

SORTING:
Sort the following 2½" strips into stacks:

POSITION	QUANTITY & COLOR	
Sashings	6	Purple
Large Flower Block	7	White
2-Flower Block	4	Blue
Stems & Leaves	4	Green
Flowers	2	Yellow
Flowers & Cornerstones	4	Pink

CUTTING:
Cut 15 Purple sashing strips 2½" x 14½".
Cut 12 Pink cornerstones 2½" x 2½".

CUTTING CHARTS:
BOTH LARGE FLOWER BLOCKS:

	Quantity	Length	Position
White	4	14½"	Flower top border
	4	10½"	Flower side borders
	8	2½"	Flower corners
	12	13"	Leaf section
Pink	8	10½"	Flower
	4	4½"	Flower
Green	2	16½"	Stem
	4	13"	Leaf section
Yellow	2	2½"	Flower center

BOTH SMALL 2-FLOWER BLOCKS:

	Quantity	Length	Position
Blue	2	14½"	Sashing between flowers
	16	2½"	Folded corners
	6	10"	Leaf sections
Yellow	8	6½"	Flower
	8	2½"	Flower center strip
Pink	4	2½"	Flower center
Green	4	8½"	Stem
	2	10"	Leaf sections

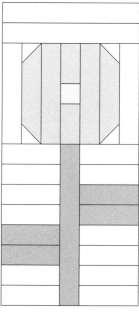

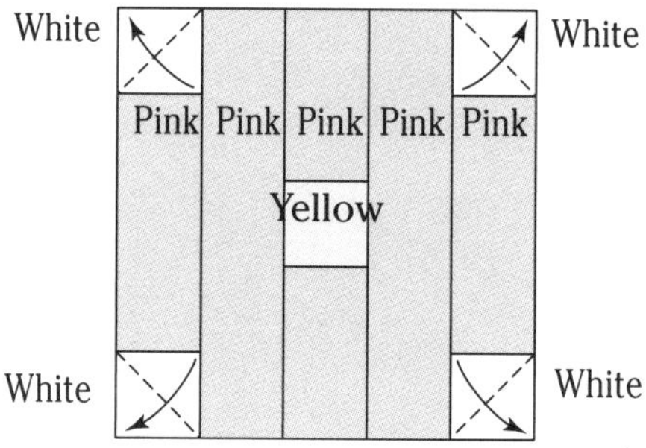

Folded Corners Diagram
for Snowball Flower

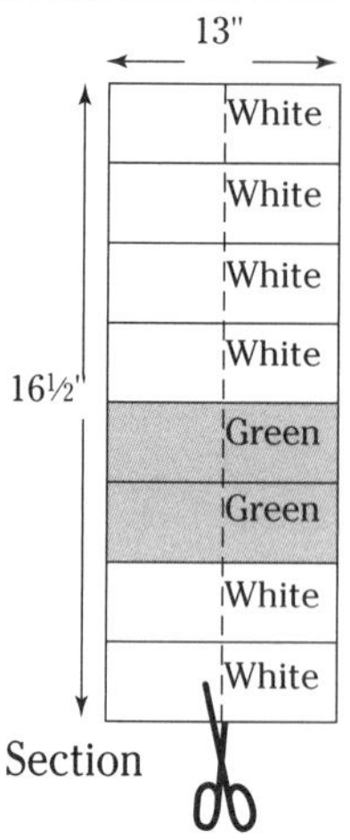

Leaf Section

Large Flower Block
Make 2

PREPARATION FOR LARGE FLOWER:
Large Flower Block:
Sew a Pink 4½" strip to each end of the
Yellow 2½" square. Press.
Sew 2 Pink 10½" strips to each side of
this center piece to make a
10½" square. Press.

Add Snowball Corners:
Refer to the Snowball Corners diagram.
Align a White 2½" square with each corner.
Noting the direction, draw a diagonal line
in each square.
Sew on the diagonal.
Fold back White to form corner triangles.
Trim away excess fabric underneath
the flower.

Add Additional Strips:
Sew a White 10½" strip to each side of
the flower. Press.
Sew 2 White 14½" strips to the top. Press.

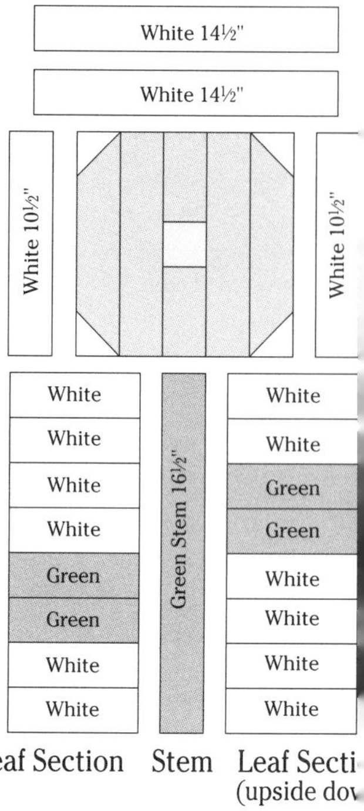

PREPARATION FOR LEAF SECTION:
Leaf Sections:
Sew 13" strips together side by side
in the following order:
4 White - 2 Green - 2 White
to make a piece 13" x 16½". Press.
Cut the piece into 2 sections,
each 6½" x 16½".

Stem and Leaf Section:
Note position of the Green leaves on Leaf Units.
Sew sections together:
Leaf Section - Green 16½" stem - Leaf
Section (upside down).
to complete the Leaf Unit. Press.

BLOCK ASSEMBLY:
Sew the Large Flower section
to the Stem and Leaf section. Press.

Repeat as above for the second flower.

Large Flower Block
Make 2

Flower Block

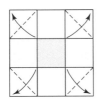
Folded Corners Diagram
Sew and Fold the Corners

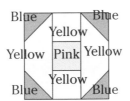
Snowball
Flower Block

mall Flowers Block
ake 2

REPARATION FOR SMALL FLOWER:

mall Flowers Block:
enter Strip - Sew a
  2½" Yellow - 2½" Pink - 2½" Yellow.
  Press.
w a 6½" Yellow to each side of this center
  strip to make a 6½" square. Press.

dd Snowball Corners:
efer to the Snowball Corners diagram.
ign a Blue 2½" square with each corner.
oting the direction, draw a diagonal line
  in each corner square.
w on the diagonal.
ld back the Blue squares to form triangles.
  Press. You will need 2 for each block.
im away excess fabric underneath.

ower Sections:
w a Flower Block to a Leaf & Stem unit.
  Press. You will need 2 for each section.

REPARATION FOR LEAF SECTION:

af Sections:
w 10" strips together side by side
  in the following order:
    Blue - Blue - Green - Blue.
  to make a piece 8½" x 10". Press.
t the piece into 4 Leaf Units,
  each 2½" x 8½".

af & Stem Sections:
ote position of the Green leaves on Leaf Units.
w sections together side by side:
    Leaf Unit - Stem - Leaf Unit
      (upside down)
  Press. You will need 2 for each section.

LOCK ASSEMBLY:
w units together:
ower Section - Blue Sashing - Flower Section.
  Press.

epeat as above for the second flower.

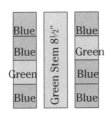
Leaf Section
Sew 4 strips
together

Cut into 4 Leaf Units

Leaf Unit   Stem   Leaf Unit
                    (upside down)

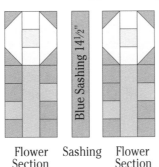
Flower   Sashing   Flower
Section   Section

Small Flowers Block - Make 2

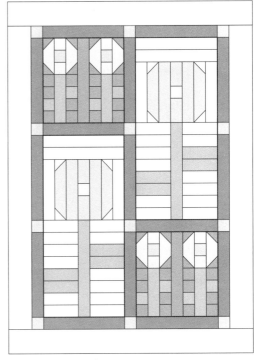
Home Garden - Quilt Assembly Diagram

ASSEMBLY:
  Sew a sashing strip to the top and bottom of
each Small Flowers block. Press.
  Column 1: Sew a Small Flowers block- Large
Flower block-Sashing. Press.
  Column 2:
  Sew a
    Sashing-Lg Flower block- Sm Flowers block.
    Press.
  Vertical Sashes:
  Sew a
  Cornerstone-Sashing-Cornerstone-Sashing-
  Cornerstone-Sashing-Cornerstone. Press.

  Make 3 strips 50½" long.
  Arrange all blocks and sashes on a work
    surface or table.
  Refer to diagram for block placement.
  Sew a
    Vertical Sashing-Column 1-Sashing-
    Column 2-Sashing. Press.

BORDER:
  Cut strips 4½" wide parallel to the selvage
    to eliminate piecing.
  Cut 2 strips 4½" x 50½" for sides.
  Cut 2 strips 4½" x 42½" for top and bottom.
  Sew side borders to the quilt. Press.
  Sew top and bottom borders to the quilt.
  Press.

FINISHING:
Quilting:
  See Basic Instructions.
Binding:
  Cut strips 2½" wide.
  Sew together end to end to equal 210".
  See Binding Instructions.

Butterfly Blocks

photo is on page 15

SIZE: 56" x 70"
TIP: Add more borders to make a larger quilt.

YARDAGE:
Yardage is given for using either fabric yardage or
    'Jelly Roll' strips.
We used a *Moda* "Butterfly Fling" by Me & My Sister
    'Jelly Roll' collection of 2½" fabric strips
    - we purchased 1 'Jelly Roll'.

10 strips	OR	¾ yard White
6 strips	OR	½ yard Lavender
6 strips	OR	½ yard Green
6 strips	OR	½ yard Pink
4 strips	OR	⅓ yard Aqua
4 strips	OR	⅓ yard Yellow

Center blocks	Purchase ½ yard Butterfly print
Border #1	Purchase ½ yard Aqua
Border #2 & Binding	Purchase 1⅞ yards Green
Backing	Purchase 3½ yards
Batting	Purchase 64" x 78"
Sewing machine, needle, thread	

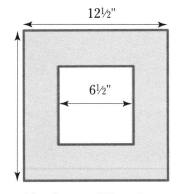

12½"

6½"

'Get Squared' Template

TIP: We used a *June Taylor* 'Get Squared' 12½" template
    with a 6½" window (or make your own from
    template plastic).

PREPARATION FOR STRIPS:
    Cut all strips 2½" by the width of fabric
        (usually 42" - 44").
    Label the stacks or pieces as you cut.

SORTING: Sort the following 2½" strips into stacks:

POSITION	QUANTITY & COLOR
Blocks 1, 8, 12	6 Lavender
Blocks 2, 9	4 Yellow
Blocks 3, 4, 11	6 Pink
Blocks 5, 10	4 Aqua
Blocks 6, 7	4 Green
Cornerstones	2 Green
Sashings	10 White

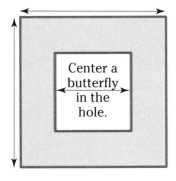

Center a butterfly in the hole.

Center a butterfly and cut a 6½" x 6½" square

CUTTING:
Center C:
    Fussy cut 12 White butterfly blocks, each block 6½" x 6½".
    Use White yardage or a panel print with 3½" butterflies .
    Position the center butterfly as close to vertical as possible.
    Refer to the Block Assembly Diagram.

Blocks: For each block, cut and label the following strips:

#1, 2	2½" x 6½"
#3, 4, 5, 6	2½" x 10½"
#7, 8	2½" x 14½"

Cornerstones: Cut 20 Green squares 2½" x 2½".
Sashings: Cut 31 White strips 2½" x 12½".

Use a 6½" x 6½" square
with a butterfly for the
center of each block.
You'll need 12.

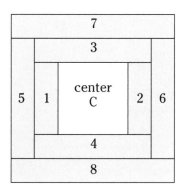

Block Assembly Diagram

BLOCK ASSEMBLY:
    Sew #1 & 2 to the left and right sides of the center C. Press.
    Sew #3 & 4 to the top and bottom of the block. Press.
    Sew #5 & 6 to the left and right sides of the block. Press.
    Sew #7 & 8 to the top and bottom of the block. Press.

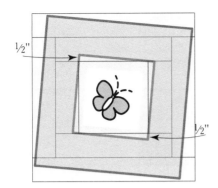

Position Template on the square
with a butterfly in the center

Position the template over the block as shown.
TIP: Notice that the upper left corner of the fussy
cut square lines up with the ½" mark on the
ruler. If you want your block to tilt in the other
direction, align the upper right corner with the
½" mark.
Trim along the outside of the template.
Each block will measure 12½" x 12½" at this point.

Finished Block

ASSEMBLY:
Refer to diagram for block placement and direction.
Rows:
For each row, sew
Sash-Block-Sash-Block-Sash-Block-Sash. Press.
Horizontal Sashings:
Make 5 of the following:
Sew Cornerstone-Sash-Cornerstone-Sash-Cornerstone-
Sash-Cornerstone. Press.
Arrange all rows and horizontal sashings on a work
surface or table.
Sew the rows together. Press.

Border #1:
Cut strips 2½" by the width of fabric.
Sew strips together end to end.
Cut 2 strips 2½" x 58½" for sides.
Cut 2 strips 2½" x 48½" for
top and bottom.
Sew side borders to the quilt. Press.
Sew top and bottom borders to the quilt.
Press.

Border #2:
Cut strips 4½" wide parallel to the selvage to
eliminate piecing.
Cut 2 strips 4½" x 62½" for sides.
Cut 2 strips 4½" x 56½" for
top and bottom.
Sew side borders to the quilt. Press.
Sew top and bottom borders to the quilt.
Press.

FINISHING:
Quilting:
See Basic Instructions.

Binding:
Cut strips 2½" wide.
Sew together end to end to equal 262".
See Binding Instructions.

Butterfly Blocks - Quilt Assembly Diagram

Fruit Salad

photo is on page 16

SIZE: 52" x 68"
TIP: Add more borders to make a larger quilt.

YARDAGE:
Yardage is given for using either fabric yardage or
   'Jelly Roll' strips.
We used a *Moda* "Recipe for Friendship" by Mary Engelbreit
   'Jelly Roll' collection of 2½" fabric strips
   - we purchased 1 'Jelly Roll'

12 strips	OR	⅞ yard White
2 strips	OR	⅙ yard Yellow
6 strips	OR	½ yard Green
7 strips	OR	⅝ yard Blue
6 strips	OR	½ yard Red
2 strips	OR	⅙ yard Black

Border #3	Purchase ⅜ yards Green
Border #4 & Binding	Purchase 1¾ yards Black Print
Backing	Purchase 3½ yards
Batting	Purchase 60" x 76"

Sewing machine, needle, thread

PREPARATION FOR STRIPS:
   Cut all strips 2½" by the width of fabric.
   Label the stacks or pieces as you cut.

SORTING - Sort the following 2½" strips into stacks:

POSITION	QUANTITY & COLOR
Applique in blocks	1 Black
	1 Green
Center of blocks	4 Red
	9 White
Border of watermelon block	3 Green
Border of heart block	2 Red
Border of cherries block	2 Black
Border of strawberry block	2 Green
Border of apple block	2 Yellow

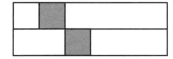

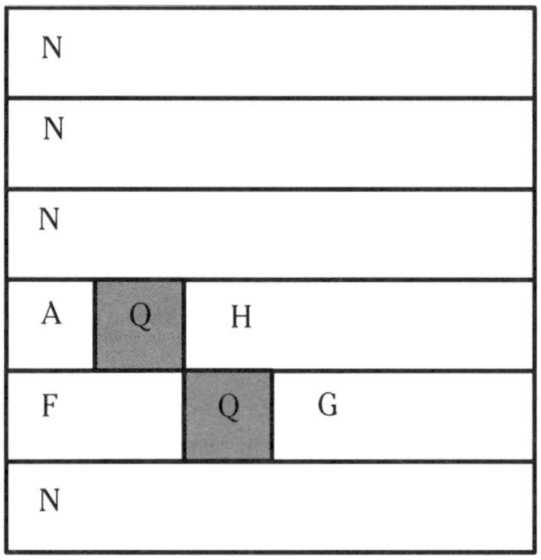

Cherry Block

Cut the following strips:

N	White	4	12½"
A	White	1	2½"
H	White	1	8½"
G	White	1	6½"
F	White	1	4½"
Q	Red	2	2½"
Black borders		2, 2	12½", 16½"

Sew Red and White strips together:
   Sew a White A, Red Q, White H together end to end.
   Sew a White F, Red Q, White G together end to end.
   Sew these 2 rows together side by side.

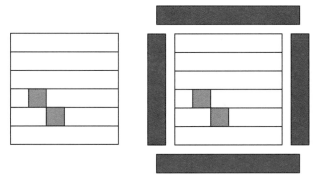

Sew remaining White strips:
   Sew 3 White N to the top of the cherries.
   Sew 1 White N to the bottom of the cherries.
   The block will measure 12½" x 12½".

Sew borders to cherry block:
   Sew Black 12½"strips to each side of the block.
   Sew Black 16½" strips to the top and bottom of
      the block.

The block will measure 16½" x 16½".

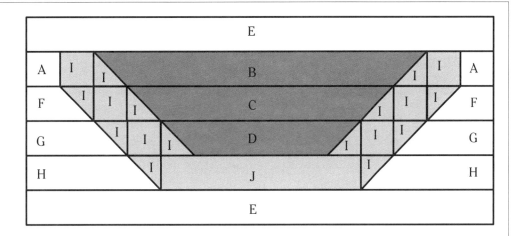

Watermelon Block

Cut the following strips:

E	White	2	28½"
H	White	2	8½"
G	White	2	6½"
F	White	2	4½"
A	White	2	2½"
B	Red	1	20½" ·
C	Red	1	16½"
D	Red	1	12½"
J	Green	1	12½"
I	Green	18	2½"
Green borders		2, 2	12½", 32½"

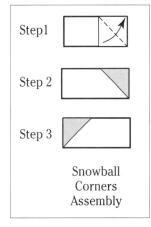

Step 1

Step 2

Step 3

Snowball
Corners
Assembly

Draw a diagonal line. Sew on the line. Fold corner back. Press.
    Cut off excess fabric from underneath.
    Repeat on the other end of Red B, being sure the diagonal is the opposite direction.

    Repeat with Green I on both ends of Red C.
    Repeat with Green I on both ends of Red D.

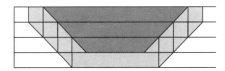

Sew Red and Green strips together:
1. Sew A - Green I - I/B/I - Green I - A. Press.
2. Sew F/I - Green I - I/C/I - Green I - I/F. Press.
3. Sew G/I - Green I - I/D/I - Green I - I/G. Press.
4. Sew H/I - J - I/H. Press.

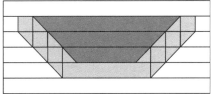

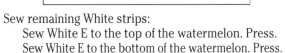

Sew remaining White strips:
    Sew White E to the top of the watermelon. Press.
    Sew White E to the bottom of the watermelon. Press.
    The block will measure 12½" x 28½".

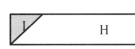

Sew Snowball Corners to the White Strips:
    Line up a Green I on one end of White F.
    Draw a diagonal line. Sew on the line.
    Fold the corner back and press.
    Cut off excess fabric from underneath.
    Repeat with the second Green I and F, being sure
        the diagonal is the opposite direction.

    Repeat with Green I on each White G.
    Repeat with Green I on each White H.

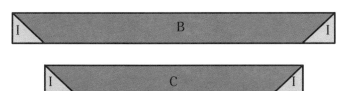

Sew Corners to the Red Strips:
    Line up a Green I on one end of Red B.

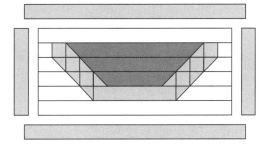

Sew borders to watermelon block:
    Sew Green 12½" strips to each side of the block. Press.
    Sew Green 32½" strips to the top and bottom of
        the block. Press.
    The block will measure 16½" x 32½".

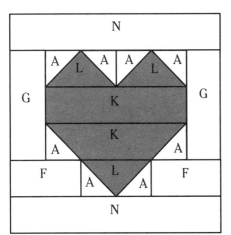

Heart Block

Cut the following strips:

N	White	2	12½"
A	White	8	2½"
G	White	2	6½"
K	Red	2	8½"
L	Red	3	4½"
F	White	2	4½"
Red borders		2	12½"
		2	16½"

Sew corners to the Red strips:

Line up a White A on one end of Red K. Draw a diagonal line. Sew on the line. Fold the corner back and press. Cut off excess fabric from underneath. Repeat on the other end of Red K, being sure diagonal is the opposite direction.

Line up a White A on one end of Red L. Draw a diagonal line, sew on the line. Fold the corner back and press. Cut off excess fabric from underneath. Repeat on the other end of Red L, being sure diagonal is the opposite direction.

Repeat with White A on 2 more of Red L.

  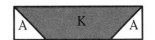

Apple Block

Cut the following strips:

N	White	2	12½"
H	White	2	8½"
A	White	6	2½"
K	Red	3	8½"
L	Red	2	4½"
Yellow borders		2	12½"
		2	16½"

Sew corners to the Red strips:

Line up a White A on one end of Red K. Draw a diagonal line. Sew on the line. Fold the corner back and press. Cut off excess fabric from underneath. Repeat on the other end of Red K, being sure diagonal is the opposite direction. Repeat with White A on 1 more Red K.

Line up a White A on one end of Red L. Draw a diagonal line, sew on the line. Fold the corner back and press. Cut off excess fabric from underneath. Repeat on the other end of Red L, being sure diagonal is the opposite direction.

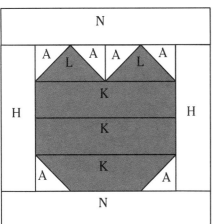

Strawberry Block

Cut the following strips:

N	White	2	12½"
G	White	2	6½"
F	White	2	4½"
A	White	6	2½"
K	Red	3	8½"
L	Red	1	4½"
Green borders		2	12½"
		2	16½"

Sew corners to the Red strips:

Line up a White A on one end of Red K. Draw a diagonal line. Sew on the line. Fold the corner back and press. Cut off excess fabric from underneath. Repeat on the other end of Red K, being sure diagonal is the opposite direction. Repeat with White As on 1 more Red K.

Line up a White A on one end of Red L. Draw a diagonal line, sew on the line. Fold the corner back and press. Cut off excess fabric from underneath. Repeat on the other end of Red L, being sure diagonal is the opposite direction.

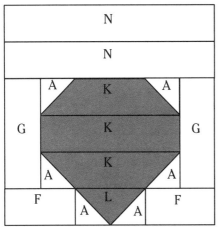

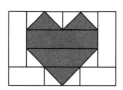

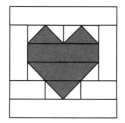

Sew Red and White strips together:
  Sew 2 White A/Red L/White A strips together end to end. Press.
  Sew 3 White/Red rows together side by side. Press.
  Sew a White G to each side of the block. Press.

  Sew 2 White F/A/Red L/White A/F together end to end. Press.
  Sew this row and the other 3 rows together side by side. Press.

Sew remaining White strips:
  Sew a White N to the top of the heart. Press.
  Sew a White N to the bottom of the heart. Press.
  The block will measure 12½" x 12½".

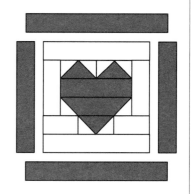

Sew borders to heart block:
  Sew Red 12½" strips to each side of the block. Press.
  Sew Red 16½" strips to the top and bottom of block. Press.

  The block will measure 16½" x 16½".

Sew Red and White strips together:
  Sew 2 White A/Red L/White A strips together end to end. Press.
  Sew 4 White/Red rows together side by side. Press.

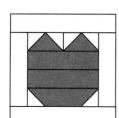

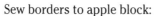

Sew remaining White strips:
  Sew White H strips to each side of the block. Press.
  Sew White N strips to the top and bottom of block. Press.
  The block will measure 12½" x 12½".

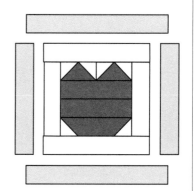

Sew borders to apple block:
  Sew Yellow 12½" strips to each side of the block. Press.
  Sew Yellow 16½" strips to the top and bottom of block. Press.

  The block will measure 16½" x 16½".

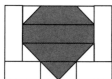
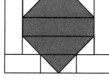

Sew Red and White strips together:
  Sew 3 White/Red rows together side by side. Press.
  Sew a White G to each side of the block. Press.
  Sew White F/A/Red L/White A/F row to the bottom of the piece. Press.

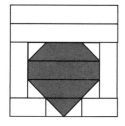

Sew remaining White strips:
  Sew 2 White N to the top of the block. Press.
  The block will measure 12½" x 12½".

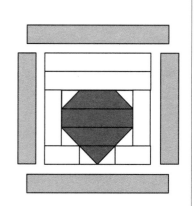

Sew borders to strawberry block:
  Sew Green 12½" strips to each side of the block. Press.
  Sew Green 16½" strips to the top and bottom of block. Press.

  The block will measure 16½" x 16½".

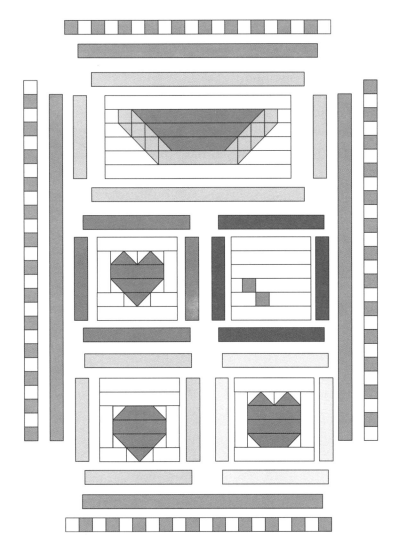

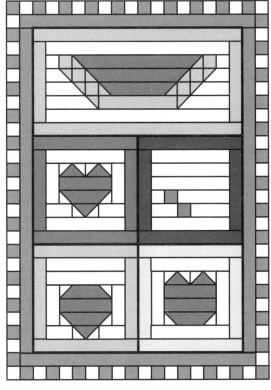

Pieced Border #1:
Cut Blue strips 2½" by the width of fabric.
Sew strips together end to end.
    Cut 2 strips 2½" x 48½" for sides.
    Cut 2 strips 2½" x 36½" for top and bottom.
    Sew side borders to the quilt. Press.
    Sew top and bottom borders to the quilt. Press.

Checkerboard Border #2:
Cut 26 strips 5" (cut 13 Blue and cut 13 White).
Sew the strips together side by side,
    alternating the Blue and White strips. Press.
    Cut the length of strips into 2 strips,
        each 2½" x 52½".
    Sew these strips to the sides of the quilt.

Cut 20 strips 5" (cut 10 Blue and cut 10 White).
Sew the strips together side by side,
    alternating the Blue and White strips. Press.
    Cut the length of strips into 2 strips,
        each 2½" x 40½".
    Sew these strips to the top and bottom
        of the quilt.

ASSEMBLY:
    Arrange all blocks on a work surface or table.
    Refer to diagram for block placement and direction.
    Sew heart block to cherry block, side by side. Press.
    Sew strawberry block to apple block, side by side. Press.

    Sew 3 rows of blocks together -
        Watermelon - Heart/Cherry - Strawberry/Apple. Press.

Stem
Cut 4 Black

Add a scant ¹/₄" around the edge for turned applique.

Leaf
Cut 3 Green
Cut 5 Black

Add a scant ¹/₄"
around the edge for
turned applique

Border #3:
Cut strips 2½" by the width of fabric.
Sew strips together end to end.
    Cut 2 strips 2½" x 56½" for sides.
    Cut 2 strips 2½" x 44½" for top and bottom.
    Sew side borders to the quilt. Press.
    Sew top and bottom borders to the quilt. Press.

Border #4:
Cut strips 4½" wide parallel to the selvage to
        eliminate piecing.
    Cut 2 strips 4½" x 60½" for sides.
    Cut 2 strips 4½" x 52½" for top and bottom.
    Sew side borders to the quilt. Press.
    Sew top and bottom borders to the quilt. Press.

FINISHING:
Quilting: See Basic Instructions.
Binding: Cut strips 2½" wide.
        Sew together end to end to equal 250".
        See Binding Instructions.

Pie, Oh My!

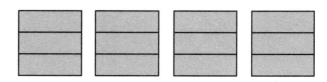

photo is on page 17

SIZE: 55" x 67"
TIP: Add more borders to make a larger quilt.

YARDAGE:
Yardage is given for using either fabric yardage or
 'Jelly Roll' strips.
We used a *Moda* "Recipe for Friendship" by Mary Engelbreit
 'Jelly Roll' collection of 2½" fabric strips
 - we purchased 1 'Jelly Roll'

6 strips	OR	½ yard Green
7 strips	OR	⅝ yard Blue
6 strips	OR	½ yard Red
2 strips	OR	⅙ yard Black
4 strips	OR	⅓ yard Yellow
12 strips	OR	⅞ yard White

Border #1 & checkerboard	Purchase ⅜ yard Blue print
Border #2	Purchase ⅓ yard White print
Border #3 & Binding	Purchase 1⅔ yards Blue print
Backing	Purchase 3⅝ yards
Batting	Purchase 63" x 75"

Sewing machine, needle, thread
DMC pearl cotton or 6-ply floss (Brown)
#22 or #24 chenille needle

PREPARATION FOR STRIPS:
 Cut all strips 2½" by the width of fabric
  (usually 42" - 44").
 Label the stacks or pieces as you cut.

SORTING:
 Sort the following 2½" strips into stacks:

POSITION		QUANTITY & COLOR	
	Applique fruit	1	Red
		leftover 16"	Green
A	Center of blocks	2	Yellow
B	Black/White border	2	Black
		2	White
C	Red border	5	Red
D	Blue border	7	Blue
E	Green/White sashing	6	Green
		6	White
F	Checkerboard border (top and bottom)		
		2	White
		2	Yellow
	use yardage from border #1		Blue

SEW STRIPS FOR A - CENTERS:
 Cut Yellow into 6 strips 13" long.
 Sew 2 sets of 3 strips together side by side. Press.
 Cut the strip set into 4 squares, each 6½" long.
 Each block will measure 6½" x 6½" at this point.

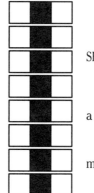

SEW STRIPS FOR B - CHECKERBOARD BORDER:
 Cut White into 4 strips 20" long.
 Cut Black into 4 strips 20" long.
 Sew 3 strips together side by side to make
a strip 20" long - White/Black/White. Press.

 Cut the strip set into 2½" wide x 6½" to
make 8 checkerboard strips.

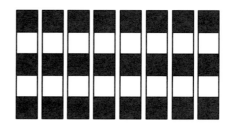

 Sew 5 strips together side by side to make a strip 20" long
- Black/White/Black/White/Black. Press.

 Cut the strip set into 2½" wide x 10½" to make 8 checkerboard strips .

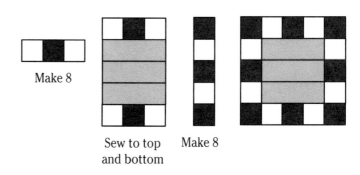

Make 8

Sew to top
and bottom

Make 8

B - SEW CHECKERBOARD BORDERS TO BLOCKS:
 Sew a 3 square border to the top and bottom of a block.
Press.
 Sew a 5 square border to each side of a block. Press.
 Each block will measure 10½" x 10½".

 Repeat to make 4 blocks.

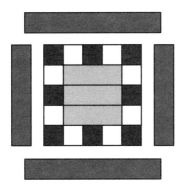

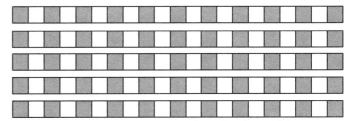

C - SEW RED BORDERS TO BLOCKS:

Cut 8 Red strips 2½" x 10½".
Cut 8 Red strips 2½" x 14½".
Sew a 10½" border to each side of a block. Press.
Sew a 14½" border to the top and bottom of a block. Press.
Each block will measure 14½" x 14½".

Repeat to make 4 blocks.

SEW STRIPS FOR HORIZONTAL SASHING B - CHECKERBOARD:

Cut White into 10 strips 12½" long.
Cut Green into 11 strips 12½" long.
Sew the 21 strips together side by side to make a strip 42½" long - begin with Green/White/Green/White/Green etc. and end with Green. Press.
Cut the strip set into 2½" wide x 42½" to make 5 checkerboard strips.

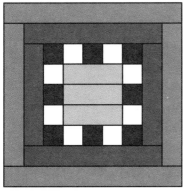

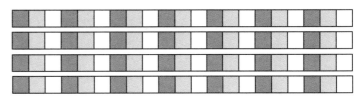

D - SEW BLUE BORDERS TO BLOCKS:

Cut 8 Blue strips 2½" x 14½".
Cut 8 Blue strips 2½" x 18½".
Sew a 14½" border to each side of a block. Press.
Sew a 18½" border to the top and bottom of a block. Press.
Each block will measure 18½" x 18½".

Repeat to make 4 blocks.

SEW STRIPS FOR TOP & BOTTOM BORDERS - CHECKERBOARD:

Cut Blue yardage (same as Border #1) into 7 strips 10" long.
Cut leftover strips (color 2) into 7 strips 10" long.
Cut leftover strips (color 3) into 7 strips 10" long.
Sew the 21 strips together side by side to make a strip 42½" long - begin with Blue/color 2/color 3/Blue//color 2/color 3, etc. Press.
Cut the strip set into 2½" wide x 42½" to make 4 checkerboard strips.

ASSEMBLE BORDERS - CHECKERBOARD:

Use 2 strip sets for the top border.
On 1 of the 3-color checkerboard strips, remove one square from the right end and sew it to the left end. Press.

Sew this new strip to a 3-color checkerboard original strip to make a 4½" wide x 42½" checkerboard border. Press.
Repeat with 2 more strip sets for the bottom border.

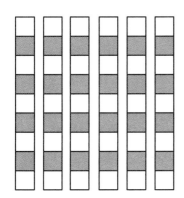

SEW STRIPS FOR VERTICAL SASHING A - CHECKERBOARD:

Cut White into 5 strips 15" long.
Cut Green into 4 strips 15" long.
Sew the 9 strips together side by side to make a strip 18½" long - begin with
White/Green/White/Green/White/etc. and end with White. Press.

Cut the strip set into 2½" wide x 18½" to make 6 checkerboard strips.

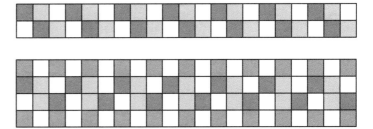

ASSEMBLE BORDERS - CHECKERBOARD:

Sew the top border by adding 2 strip sets of Sashing B to a 4½" wide x 42½" checkerboard border:

Row 1 - Sashing B/Checkerboard/Sashing B. Press.

Row 5 - Repeat for the bottom border. Press.

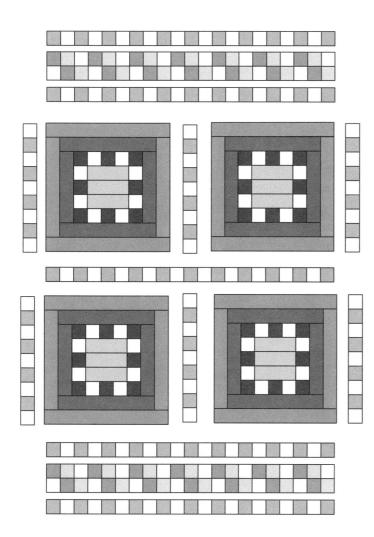

ASSEMBLY:
Arrange all blocks on a work surface or table.
Refer to diagram for block placement and direction.
Sew blocks together in 5 rows:

Row 2 -
Sashing A/Cherry block/Sashing A/Apple block/Sashing A.

Row 4 -
Sashing A/Strawberry block/Sashing A/Heart block/Sashing A.
Press.

Center Section - Sew the 3 center rows together:
Row 1/Row 2/Sashing B/Row4/Row 5. Press.
You have completed the center section.

BORDERS:
Inner Border #1:
Cut 6 Blue strips 1½" by the width of fabric.
Sew strips together end to end.
Cut 2 strips 1½" x 54½" for sides.
Cut 2 strips 1½" x 44½" for top and bottom.
Sew side borders to the quilt. Press.
Sew top and bottom borders to the quilt. Press.

Middle Border #2:
Cut 6 White plaid strips 1½" by the width of fabric.
Sew strips together end to end.
Cut 2 strips 1½" x 56½" for sides.
Cut 2 strips 1½" x 46½" for top and bottom.
Sew side borders to the quilt. Press.
Sew top and bottom borders to the quilt. Press.

Outer Border #3:
Cut strips 4½" wide parallel to the selvage to
eliminate piecing.
Cut 2 strips 4½" x 58½" for sides.
Cut 2 strips 4½" x 54½" for top and bottom.
Sew side borders to the quilt. Press.
Sew top and bottom borders to the quilt. Press.

FINISHING:
Quilting:
See Basic Instructions.
Binding:
Cut strips 2½" wide.
Sew together end to end to equal 254".
See Binding Instructions.

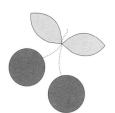

Leaf
Cut 2 Green
Add a scant $1/4$"
around the edge
for turned
applique.

Cherry
Cut 2 Red

Add a scant $1/4$"
around the edge for
turned applique.

Leaf
Cut 1 Green
Add a scant $1/4$" around
the edge for turned
applique.

Apple
Cut 1 Red

Add a scant $1/4$"
around the edge for
turned applique.

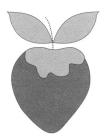

Leaf
Cut 2 Green
Add a scant $1/4$"
around the edge for
turned applique.

Top of Strawberry
Cut 1 Green
Add a scant $1/4$"
around the edge for
turned applique.

Strawberry
Cut 1 Red

Add a scant $1/4$"
around the edge for
turned applique.

Heart
Cut 1 Red

Add a scant $1/4$"
around the edge for
turned applique.

The Best Things About 'Jelly Rolls'

I love to quilt, but it is often difficult to find time to cut and piece a quilt top. When I saw collections of 2¹/₂" pre-cut fabric strips, I knew they were the answer.

No more spending hours choosing and cutting fabrics. Now I can begin sewing right away. Beautiful colors are available in every set. So whether I like jewel colors, heritage patterns, soft pastels or earthy tones... there is an assortment for me.

Now my goals... a handmade cover for every bed, an heirloom quilt for each new baby and a pieced quilt for each of my children... are within reach. With 'Jelly Rolls' it is possible to complete a quilt top in a weekend.

After I piece all the blocks together, I use leftover strips for the borders and binding. Nothing really goes to waste and, if needed, I can purchase a bit of extra fabric for an extra punch of color or an additional yard for the border.

TIP: Quantities are given in strips and yardage so you know what you need and can start right away.

Tips for Working with Strips

Guide for Yardage:

2¹/₂" Strips - Each ¼ yard or a 'Fat Quarter' equals 3 strips - A pre-cut 'Jelly Roll' strip is 2½" x 44"

Pre-cut strips are cut on the crosswise grain and are prone to stretching. These tips will help reduce stretching and make your quilt lay flat for quilting.

1. If you are cutting yardage, cut on the grain. Cut fat quarters on grain, parallel to the 18" side.

2. When sewing crosswise grain strips together, take care not to stretch the strips. If you detect any puckering as you go, rip out the seam and sew it again.

3. Press, Do Not Iron. Carefully open fabric, with the seam to one side, press without moving the iron. A back-and-forth ironing motion stretches the fabric.

4. Reduce the wiggle in your borders with this technique from garment making. First, accurately cut your borders to the exact measure of the quilt top. Then, before sewing the border to the quilt, run a double row of stay stitches along the outside edge to maintain the original shape and prevent stretching. Pin the border to the quilt, taking care not to stretch the quilt top to make it fit. Pinning reduces slipping and stretching.

Rotary Cutting

Rotary Cutter: Friend or Foe

A rotary cutter is wonderful and useful. When not used correctly, the sharp blade can be a dangerous tool. Follow these safety tips:

1. Never cut toward you.

2. Use a sharp blade. Pressing harder on a dull blade can cause the blade to jump the ruler and injure your fingers.

3. Always disengage the blade before the cutter leaves your hand, even if you intend to pick it up immediately.

Rotary cutters have been caught when lifting fabric, have fallen onto the floor and have cut fingers.

Basic Sewing

You now have precisely cut strips that are exactly the correct width. You are well on your way to blocks that fit together perfectly. Accurate sewing is the next important step.

Matching Edges:

1. Carefully line up the edges of your strips. Many times, if the underside is off a little, your seam will be off by $1/8$". This does not sound like much until you have 8 seams in a block, each off by $1/8$". Now your finished block is a whole inch wrong!

2. Pin the pieces together to prevent them shifting.

Seam Allowance:

I cannot stress enough the importance of accurate $1/4$" seams. All the quilts in this book are measured for $1/4$" seams unless otherwise indicated.

Most sewing machine manufacturers offer a Quarter-inch foot. A Quarter-inch foot is the most worthwhile investment you can make in your quilting.

Pressing:

I want to talk about pressing even before we get to sewing because proper pressing can make the difference between a quilt that wins a ribbon at the quilt show and one that does not.

Press, do NOT iron. What does that mean? Many of us want to move the iron back and forth along the seam. This "ironing" stretches the strip out of shape and creates errors that accumulate as the quilt is constructed. Believe it or not, there is a correct way to press your seams, and here it is:

1. Do NOT use steam with your iron. If you need a little water, spritz it on.

2. Place your fabric flat on the ironing board without opening the seam. Set a hot iron on the seam and count to 3. Lift the iron and move to the next position along the seam. Repeat until the entire seam is pressed. This sets and sinks the threads into the fabric.

3. Now, carefully lift the top strip and fold it away from you so the seam is on one side. Usually the seam is pressed toward the darker fabric, but often the direction of the seam is determined by the piecing requirements.

4. Press the seam open with your fingers. Add a little water or spray starch if it wants to close again. Lift the iron and place it on the seam. Count to 3. Lift the iron again and continue until the seam is pressed. Do NOT

use the tip of the iron to push the seam open. So many people do this and wonder later why their blocks are not fitting together.

5. Most critical of all: For accuracy every seam must be pressed before the next seam is sewn.

Working with 'Crosswise Grain' Strips:

Strips cut on the crosswise grain (from selvage to selvage) have problems similar to bias edges and are prone to stretching. To reduce stretching and make your quilt lay flat for quilting, keep these tips in mind.

1. Take care not to stretch the strips as you sew.

2. Adjust the sewing thread tension and the presser foot pressure if needed.

3. If you detect any puckering as you go, rip out the seam and sew it again. It is much easier to take out a seam now than to do it after the block is sewn.

Sewing Bias Edges:

Bias edges wiggle and stretch out of shape very easily. They are not recommended for beginners, but even a novice can accomplish bias edges if these techniques are employed.

1. Stabilize the bias edge with one of these methods:

a) Press with spray starch.

b) Press freezer paper or removable iron-on stabilizer to the back of the fabric.

c) Sew a double row of stay stitches along the bias edge and $1/8$" from the bias edge. This is a favorite technique of garment makers.

2. Pin, pin, pin! I know many of us dislike pinning, but when working with bias edges, pinning makes the difference between intersections that match and those that do not.

Building Better Borders:

Wiggly borders make a quilt very difficult to finish. However, wiggly borders can be avoided with these techniques.

1. Cut the borders on grain. That means cutting your strips parallel to the selvage edge.

2. Accurately cut your borders to the exact measure of the quilt.

3. If your borders are piece stripped from crosswise grain fabrics, press well with spray starch and sew a double row of stay stitches along the outside edge to maintain the original shape and prevent stretching.

4. Pin the border to the quilt, taking care not to stretch the quilt top to make it fit. Pinning reduces slipping and stretching.

Embroidery Use 24" lengths of doubled pearl cotton or 6-ply floss and a #22 or #24 Chenille needle (this needle has a large eye). Outline large elements.

Running Stitch Come up at A. Weave the needle through the fabric, making LONG stitches on the top and SHORT stitches on the bottom. Keep stitches even.

Applique Instructions

Basic Turned Edge

1. Trace pattern onto no-melt template plastic (or onto Wash-Away Tear-Away Stabilizer).

2. Cut out the fabric shape leaving a scant $\frac{1}{4}$" fabric border all around and clip the curves.

3. **Plastic Template Method -** Place plastic shape on the wrong side of the fabric. Spray edges with starch. Press a $\frac{1}{4}$" border over the edge of the template plastic with the tip of a hot iron. Press firmly.

Stabilizer Method - Place stabilizer shape on the wrong dside of the fabric. Use a glue stick to press a $\frac{1}{4}$" border over the edge of the stabilizer securing it with the glue stick. Press firmly.

5. Remove the template, maintaining the folded edge on the back of the fabric.

6. Position the shape on the quilt and Blindstitch in place.

Basic Turned Edge by Hand

1. Cut out the shape leaving a $\frac{1}{4}$" fabric border all around.

2. Baste the shapes to the quilt, keeping the basting stitches away from the edge of the fabric.

3. Begin with all areas that are under other layers and work to the topmost layer.

4. For an area no more than 2" ahead of where you are working, trim to $\frac{1}{8}$" and clip the curves.

5. Using the needle, roll the edge under and sew tiny Blindstitches to secure.

Using Fusible Web for Iron-on Applique:

1. Trace pattern onto Steam a Seam 2 fusible web.

2. Press the patterns onto the wrong side of fabric.

3. Cut out patterns exactly on the drawn line.

4. Score web paper with a pin, then remove the paper.

5. Position the fabric, fusible side down, on the quilt. Press with a hot iron following the fusible web manufacturer's instructions.

6. Stitch around the edge by hand.

Optional: Stabilize the wrong side of the fabric with your favorite stabilizer.

Use a size 80 machine embroidery needle. Fill the bobbin with lightweight basting thread and thread machine with machine embroidery thread that complements the color being appliqued.

Set your machine for a Zigzag stitch and adjust the thread tension if needed. Use a scrap to experiment with different stitch widths and lengths until you find the one you like best.

Sew slowly.

Basic Layering Instructions

Marking Your Quilt:

If you choose to mark your quilt for hand or machine quilting, it is much easier to do so before layering. Press your quilt before you begin. Here are some handy tips regarding marking.

1. A disappearing pen may vanish before you finish.

2. Use a White pencil on dark fabrics.

3. If using a washable Blue pen, remember that pressing may make the pen permanent.

Pieced Backings:

1. Press the backing fabric before measuring.

2. If possible cut backing fabrics on grain, parallel to the selvage edges.

3. Piece 3 parts rather than 2 whenever possible, sewing 2 side borders to the center. This reduces stress on the pieced seam.

4. Backing and batting should extend at least 2" on each side of the quilt.

Creating a Quilt Sandwich:

1. Press the backing and top to remove all wrinkles.

2. Lay the backing wrong side up on the table.

3. Position the batting over the backing and smooth out all wrinkles.

4. Center the quilt top over the batting leaving a 2" border all around.

5. Pin the layers together with 2" safety pins positioned a handwidth apart. A grapefruit spoon makes inserting the pins easier. Leaving the pins open in the container speeds up the basting on the next quilt.

Basic Quilting Instructions

Hand Quilting:

Many quilters enjoy the serenity of hand quilting. Because the quilt is handled a great deal, it is important to securely baste the sandwich together. Place the quilt in a hoop and don't forget to hide your knots.

Machine Quilting:

All the quilts in this book were machine quilted. Some were quilted on a large, free-arm quilting machine and others were quilted on a sewing machine. If you have never machine quilted before, practice on some scraps first.

Straight Line Machine Quilting Tips:

1. Pin baste the layers securely.

2. Set up your sewing machine with a size 80 quilting needle and a walking foot.

3. Experimenting with the decorative stitches on your machine adds interest to your quilt. You do not have to quilt the entire piece with the same stitch. Variety is the spice of life, so have fun trying out stitches you have never used before as well as your favorite stand-bys.

Free Motion Machine Quilting Tips:

1. Pin baste the layers securely.

2. Set up your sewing machine with a spring needle, a quilting foot, and lower the feed dogs.

Basic Mitered Binding

A Perfect Finish:

The binding endures the most stress on a quilt and is usually the first thing to wear out. For this reason, we recommend using a double fold binding.

1. Trim the backing and batting even with the quilt edge.

2. If possible cut strips on the crosswise grain because a little bias in the binding is a Good thing. This is the only place in the quilt where bias is helpful, for it allows the binding to give as it is turned to the back and sewn in place.

3. Strips are usually cut $2\frac{1}{2}$" wide, but check the instructions for your project before cutting.

4. Sew strips end to end to make a long strip sufficient to go all around the quilt plus 4"- 6".

5. With wrong sides together, fold the strip in half lengthwise. Press.

6. Stretch out your hand and place your little finger at the corner of the quilt top. Place the binding where your thumb touches the edge of the quilt. Aligning the edge of the quilt with the raw edges of the binding, pin the binding in place along the first side.

7. Leaving a 2" tail for later use, begin sewing the binding to the quilt with a $\frac{1}{4}$" seam.

For Mitered Corners:

1. Stop $\frac{1}{4}$" from the first corner. Leave the needle in the quilt and turn it 90°. Hit the reverse button on your machine and back off the quilt leaving the threads connected.

2. Fold the binding perpendicular to the side you sewed, making a 45° angle. Carefully maintaining the first fold, bring the binding back along the edge to be sewn.

3. Carefully align the edges of the binding with the quilt edge and sew as you did the first side. Repeat this process until you reach the tail left at the beginning. Fold the tail out of the way and sew until you are $\frac{1}{4}$" from the beginning stitches.

4. Remove the quilt from the machine. Fold the quilt out of the way and match the binding tails together. Carefully sew the binding tails with a $\frac{1}{4}$" seam. You can do this by hand if you prefer.

Finishing the Binding:

5. Trim the seam to reduce bulk.

6. Finish stitching the binding to the quilt across the join you just sewed.

7. Turn the binding to the back of the quilt. To reduce bulk at the corners, fold the miter in the opposite direction from which it was folded on the front.

8. Hand-sew a Blind stitch on the back of the quilt to secure the binding in place.

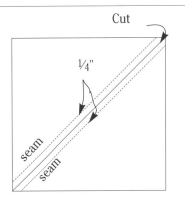

Half-Square Triangle

1. Place 2 squares right sides together.
2. Draw a diagonal line from corner to corner.
3. Stitch $\frac{1}{4}$" on each side of the line.
4. Cut squares apart on the diagonal line.
5. Open the 2 new squares with 2 colors.
6. Press. Trim off dog-ears.
7. Center and trim to size.

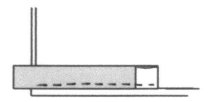

Align the raw edge of the binding with the raw edge of the quilt top. Start about 8" from the corner and go along the first side with a $\frac{1}{4}$" seam.

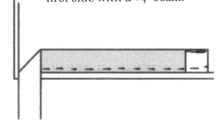

Stop $\frac{1}{4}$" from the edge. Then stitch a slant to the corner (through both layers of binding)... lift up, then down, as you line up the edge. Fold the binding back.

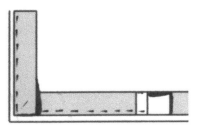

Align the raw edge again. Continue stitching the next side with a $\frac{1}{4}$" seam as you sew the binding in place.

Woodlands

photo is on page 83

SIZE: 68" x 74"
TIP: Add more borders to make a larger quilt.

YARDAGE:

Yardage is given for using either fabric yardage or
  'Jelly Roll' strips.
We used a *Moda* "Pine Creek Crossing" by Holly Taylor
  'Jelly Roll' collection of 2½" fabric strips
  - we purchased 1 'Jelly Roll'

8 strips	OR	⅝ yard Tan
7 strips	OR	½ yard Gold
8 strips	OR	⅝ yard Black
5 strips	OR	⅜ yard Green
4 strips	OR	⅓ yard Cream
3 strips	OR	¼ yard Brown
2 strips	OR	⅙ yard Rust

Border #3	Purchase ½ yard Tan
Border #2, #4 & Binding	Purchase 2⅛ yards Black
Backing	Purchase 4¼ yards
Batting	Purchase 76" x 82"

Sewing machine, needle, thread
5 Black ½" buttons
DMC pearl cotton or 6-ply floss
#22 or #24 chenille needle

PREPARATION FOR STRIPS:

Cut all strips 2½" by the width of fabric
  (usually 42" - 44").
Label the stacks or pieces as you cut.

SORTING: Sort the 2½" strips into stacks.

POSITION	QUANTITY & COLOR
Blocks A, D, F, H & Sashing	7 Gold
Blocks C, E, H & Sashing	5 Green
Blocks B, C, F	4 Cream
Blocks A, C, D, H, I	3 Brown
Blocks B, G	2 Rust
Blocks F, G, I & Sashing	4 Black
Blocks D, E, G, I & Sashing	7 Tan

CUTTING CHART FOR SASHING:

	Quantity	Length	Position
Green	2	30½"	D, L
	1	18½"	J
	1	16½"	O
	1	14½"	A
Black	2	18½"	H, K
	1	16½"	P
	1	14½"	B
	1	12½"	E
Tan	1	18½"	I
	2	16½"	M, N
	2	12½"	F, G
Gold	1	16½"	Q
	1	14½"	C

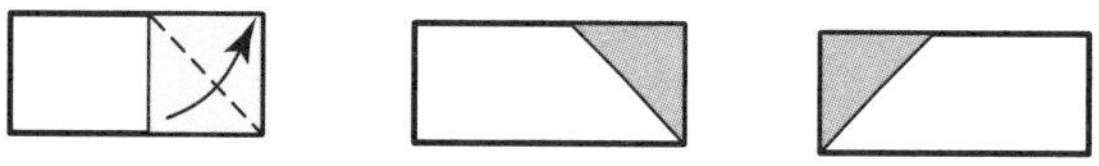

Snowball Corner Diagram

SNOWBALL CORNERS:

Some strips in the blocks use the Snowball Corner technique. The direction of the diagonal for each strip in the block varies, so you must carefully note the diagonal on the block assembly diagram. Some strips have a corner on only one end. The squares used as Snowball Corners are labelled with a "c" in the cutting list.

Tip: Fold back the triangle and check its position before you sew.

Align a square with the appropriate end of the strip and sew on the diagonal line. Fold the triangle back and press before attaching it to any other strips.

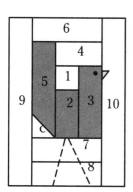

BIRD – BLOCK B
CUTTING CHART

	Quantity	Length	Position
Cream	2	14½"	#9, 10
	3	6½"	#6, 7, 8
	1	4½"	#4
	2	2½"	#1, "c"
Rust	1	8½"	#5
	1	6½"	#3
	1	4½"	#2
Gold	1	1½"	Beak applique

ASSEMBLY:

Refer to the Snowball Corners instructions.
Sew Snowball square "c" to strip 5. Press.
Sew 1-2. Press.
Sew 1-2 to 3. Press.
Sew 4 to the top of the piece. Press.
Sew 5 to the left side of the piece. Press.
Sew 6 to the top of the piece. Press.
Sew 7-8. Press.
Sew 7-8 to the bottom of the piece. Press.
Sew 9 & 10 to the left and right sides of the piece. Press.
Fold a Gold 1½" square into a beak shape (page 37).
Applique in place.
Embroider the legs with a long and short Running stitch.

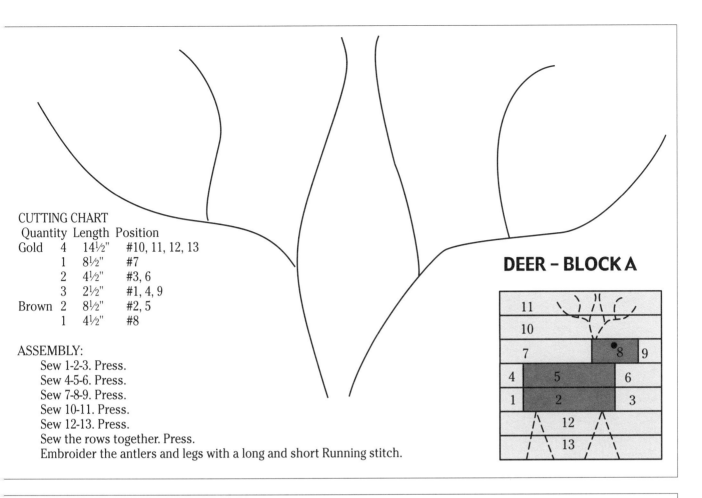

DEER – BLOCK A

CUTTING CHART

	Quantity	Length	Position
Gold	4	14½"	#10, 11, 12, 13
	1	8½"	#7
	2	4½"	#3, 6
	3	2½"	#1, 4, 9
Brown	2	8½"	#2, 5
	1	4½"	#8

ASSEMBLY:

Sew 1-2-3. Press.
Sew 4-5-6. Press.
Sew 7-8-9. Press.
Sew 10-11. Press.
Sew 12-13. Press.
Sew the rows together. Press.
Embroider the antlers and legs with a long and short Running stitch.

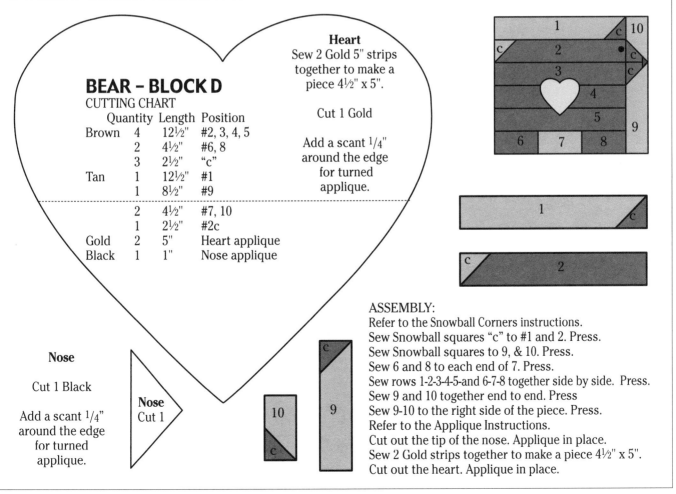

BEAR – BLOCK D

CUTTING CHART

	Quantity	Length	Position
Brown	4	12½"	#2, 3, 4, 5
	2	4½"	#6, 8
	3	2½"	"c"
Tan	1	12½"	#1
	1	8½"	#9
	2	4½"	#7, 10
	1	2½"	#2c
Gold	2	5"	Heart applique
Black	1	1"	Nose applique

Heart
Sew 2 Gold 5" strips together to make a piece 4½" x 5".

Cut 1 Gold

Add a scant ¼" around the edge for turned applique.

Nose

Cut 1 Black

Add a scant ¼" around the edge for turned applique.

Nose
Cut 1

ASSEMBLY:
Refer to the Snowball Corners instructions.
Sew Snowball squares "c" to #1 and 2. Press.
Sew Snowball squares to 9, & 10. Press.
Sew 6 and 8 to each end of 7. Press.
Sew rows 1-2-3-4-5-and 6-7-8 together side by side. Press.
Sew 9 and 10 together end to end. Press
Sew 9-10 to the right side of the piece. Press.
Refer to the Applique Instructions.
Cut out the tip of the nose. Applique in place.
Sew 2 Gold strips together to make a piece 4½" x 5".
Cut out the heart. Applique in place.

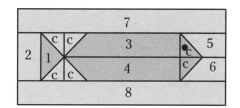

FISH – BLOCK E
CUTTING CHART

	Quantity	Length	Position
Tan	2	18½"	#7, 8
	3	4½"	#2, 5, 6
	4	2½"	"c"
Green	2	10½"	#3, 4
	1	4½"	#1
	2	2½"	#5c, 6c

ASSEMBLY:
Refer to the Snowball Corners instructions.
Sew Snowball squares "c" to
   #1, 3, 4, 5, & 6. Press.
Sew 1-2. Press.
Sew 3-4. Press.
Sew 5-6. Press.
Sew 1-2 to 3-4 to 5-6. Press.
Sew 7 & 8 to the top and
   bottom of the piece. Press.

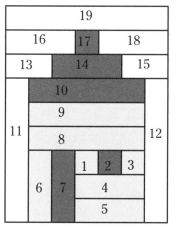

HUNTING LODGE BLOCK F
CUTTING CHART

	Quantity	Length	Position
Gold	2	10½"	#8, 9
	3	6½"	#4, 5, 6
	2	2½"	#1, 3
Black	1	10½"	#10
	2	6½"	#7, 14
	2	2½"	#2, 17
Cream	1	14½"	#19
	2	12½"	#11, 12
	2	6½"	#16, 18
	2	4½"	#13, 15

ASSEMBLY:
Sew 1-2-3 together. Press.
   Sew 4-5 together side by side. Press.
   Sew 4-5 to the bottom of 1-2-3. Press.
   Sew 6-7. Press.
   Sew 6-7 to the left side of the piece. Press.
   Sew 8-9-10. Press.
   Sew 8-9-10 to the top of the piece. Press.
Sew 11 & 12 to the left and right sides of the piece.
   Press.
   Sew 13-14-15. Press.
   Sew 16-17-18. Press.
   Sew the rows together. Press.

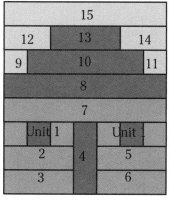

CABIN – BLOCK G
CUTTING CHART

	Quantity	Length	Position
Black	1	14½"	#8
	1	10½"	#10
	2	6½"	#4, 13
	1	5"	Unit 1
Tan	1	14½"	#15
	2	4½"	#12, 14
	2	2½"	#9, 11
Rust	1	14½"	#7
	4	6½"	#2, 3, 5, 6
	2	5"	Unit 1

ASSEMBLY:
Window Unit 1:
Refer to the Unit 1
  diagram. Sew
  Rust-Black-Rust
  strips together to make
  a piece 5" x 6½". Press.
  Cut the piece into 2
  units, each 2½" x 6½".
Cabin:
Sew Unit 1-2-3. Press.
  Sew Unit 1-5-6. Press.
  Sew 1-2-3 to 4 to 1-5-6. Press.
  Sew 9-10-11. Press.
  Sew 12-13-14. Press.
  Sew the rows together. Press.

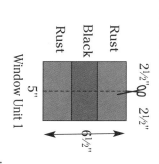

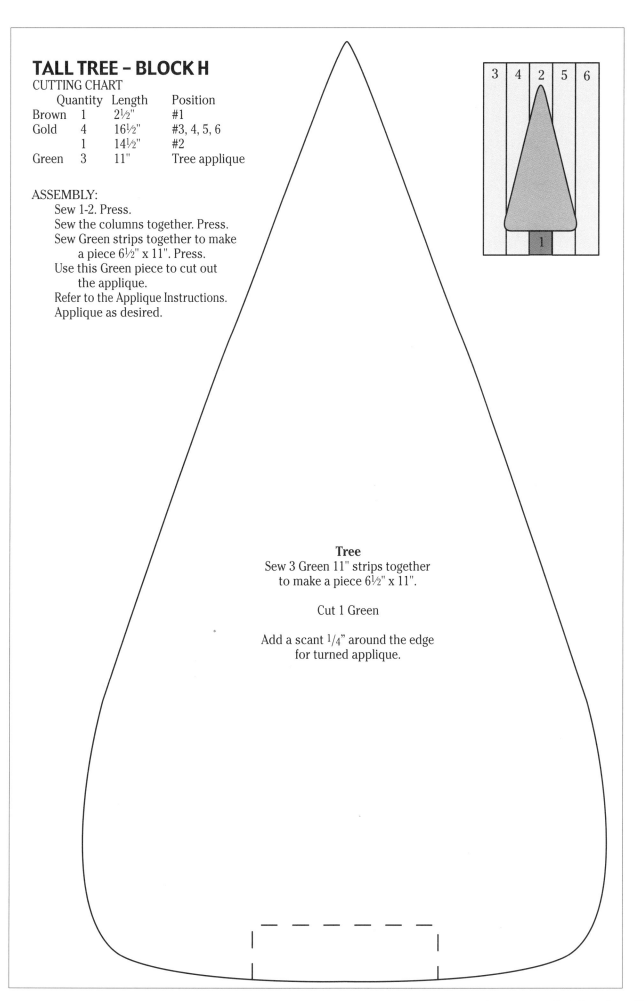

TALL TREE – BLOCK H
CUTTING CHART

	Quantity	Length	Position
Brown	1	2½"	#1
Gold	4	16½"	#3, 4, 5, 6
	1	14½"	#2
Green	3	11"	Tree applique

ASSEMBLY:

Sew 1-2. Press.
Sew the columns together. Press.
Sew Green strips together to make
    a piece 6½" x 11". Press.
Use this Green piece to cut out
    the applique.
Refer to the Applique Instructions.
Applique as desired.

Tree
Sew 3 Green 11" strips together
to make a piece 6½" x 11".

Cut 1 Green

Add a scant ¹/₄" around the edge
for turned applique.

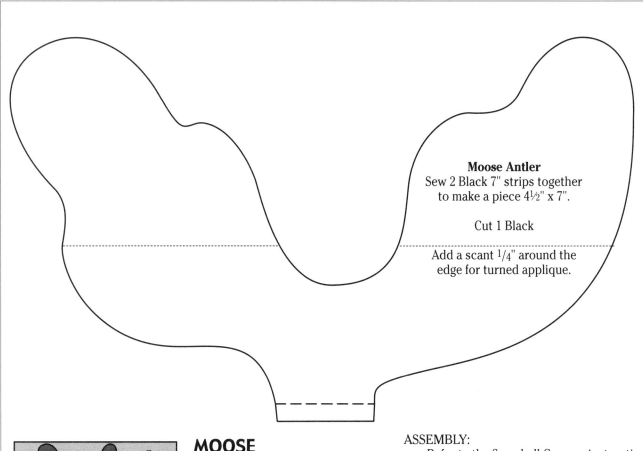

Moose Antler
Sew 2 Black 7" strips together
to make a piece 4½" x 7".

Cut 1 Black

Add a scant ¹/₄" around the
edge for turned applique.

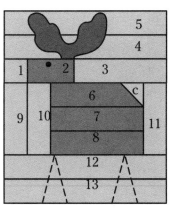

MOOSE BLOCK I

CUTTING CHART

	Quantity	Length	Position
Tan	4	14½"	#4, 5, 12, 13
	1	8½"	#3
	3	6½"	#9, 10, 11
	2	2½"	#1, 6c
Brown	3	8½"	#6, 7, 8
	1	4½"	#2
Black	2	7"	Antler applique

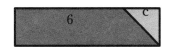

ASSEMBLY:
Refer to the Snowball Corners instructions.
Sew Snowball square "c" to #6. Press.
Top Section: Sew 1-2-3. Press.
Sew 4-5. Press.
Sew 4-5 to the top of 1-2-3. Press.
Bottom Section: Sew 6-7-8. Press.
Sew 9-10. Press.
Sew 9-10 to the left side of the piece. Press.
Sew 11 to the right side of the piece. Press.
Sew 12-13. Press.
Sew 12-13 to the bottom of the piece. Press.
Sew top and bottom sections together. Press.
Applique: Refer to the Applique Instructions.
Sew 2 Black strips together for moose rack.
Applique as desired.

SMALL TREE – BLOCK C

CUTTING CHART

	Quantity	Length	Position
Brown	1	2½"	#10
Green	3	6½"	#1, 2, 3
	1	4½"	#7
Cream	1	10½"	#12
	2	6½"	#4, 5
	2	4½"	#9, 11
	2	3½"	#6, 8
	8	2½"	"c"

ASSEMBLY:
Refer to the Snowball Corners
  instructions.
Sew Snowball squares "c" to each
  end of #1, 2, 3, & 7. Press.
Sew 1-2-3 together side by side.
  Press.
Sew 4 & 5 to the left and right side
  of the piece. Press.
Sew 6-7-8. Press.
Sew 9-10-11. Press.
  Sew the rows together. Press.

Make 1

Make 3

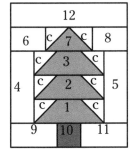

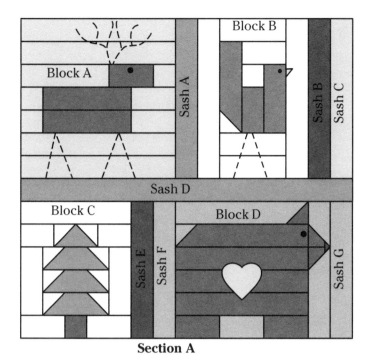

Section A

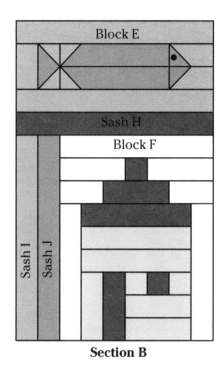

Section B

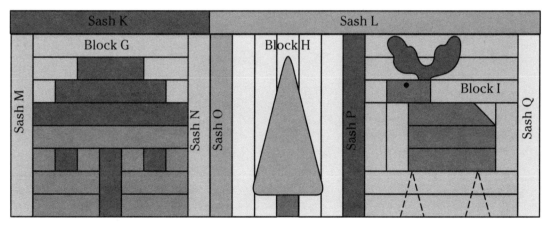

Section C

ASSEMBLY:
Arrange all blocks on a work surface or table.
Refer to diagram for block placement and direction.
Section A:
  Row 1: Sew Block A-Sash A-Block B-Sashes B & C. Press.
    Sew Sash D to the bottom of the piece. Press.
  Row 2: Sew Block C-Sashes E & F- Block D- Sash G. Press.
    Sew rows together. Press.
Section B:
  Row 1: Sew Sashing H to the bottom of Block F. Press.
  Row 2: Sew Sashes I & J to the left side of Block F. Press.
  Sew the rows together. Press.
  Sew Sections A and B together. Press.

Section C: Sew Sash M-Block G-Sashes N & O- Block H- Sash P- Block I- Sash Q. Press.
    Sew Sash K-Sash L. Press.
    Sew Sash K-L to the top if the piece. Press.
    Sew Section C to the bottom of Section A-B. Press.

Woodlands - Quilt Assembly Diagram

Suppliers - Most quilt and fabric stores carry an excellent assortment of supplies. If you need something special, ask your local store to contact the following companies.

FABRICS, 'JELLY ROLLS', 'FAT QUARTERS'
   Moda and United Notions,
   Dallas, TX, 972-484-8901

QUILTERS
   Susan Corbett, 817-361-7762
   Julie Lawson, 817-428-5929
   Sue Needle, 817-589-1168

MANY THANKS to my staff for their cheerful help and wonderful ideas!
Kathy Mason • Patty Williams
Donna Kinsey • Janet Long
David & Donna Thomason

BORDERS:

Pieced Border #1:

From remaining strips and border #4 fabric, cut Black strips 2½" by the width of fabric.
Sew strips together end to end.
   Cut 2 strips 2½" x 46½" for sides.
   Cut 2 strips 2½" x 52½" for top and bottom.
   Sew side borders to the quilt. Press.
   Sew top and bottom borders to the quilt. Press.

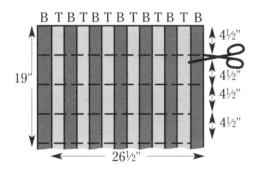

Piano Key Border #2

Piano Key Border #2:

Refer to the Piano Key diagram.
Cut 7 Black and 6 Tan strips 2½" x 19".
   Sew strips together B-T-B-T-B-T-B-T-B-T-B-T-B to make a piece 19" x 26½". Press.
   Cut the piece into 4 Strip units, each 4½" x 26½".
   Sew a 2 Strip units end to end to make a border strip 4½" x 52½". Press. Make 2.
   Sew a strip to the top and bottom of the quilt. Press.

Border #3:

Cut strips 2½" by the width of fabric.
Sew strips together end to end.
   Cut 2 strips 2½" x 62½" for sides.
   Cut 2 strips 2½" x 52½" for top and bottom.
   Sew top and bottom borders to the quilt. Press.
   Sew side borders to the quilt. Press.

Border #4:

Cut strips 6½" wide parallel to the selvage to eliminate piecing.
   Cut 2 strips 6½" x 62½" for sides.
   Cut 2 strips 6½" x 68½" for top and bottom.
   Sew side borders to the quilt. Press.
   Sew top and bottom borders to the quilt. Press.

FINISHING:

Applique:
   See Basic Instructions.
   Cut out pieces from patterns. Applique as desired.
   Embroider the legs with a long and short Running stitch.

Quilting:
   See Basic Instructions.

Binding:
   Cut strips 2½" wide.
   Sew together end to end to equal 294".
   See Binding Instructions.

Sew a button for the eye on the deer, bird, fish, and moose.